PRAISE

When I read a business book that is refreshingly free of business jargon it is always a sign that the author is very confident in their subject. This is a clear well-written dose of common sense derived from Richard's many years of experience. Anyone already involved in retail and anyone contemplating a career or business in retail should read this.

Nick Jenkins – Founder of Moonpig and former Dragon on the BBC's Dragons' Den

After looking at the economics behind thousands of retail businesses I understand the pressures they face. This book is perfect for an entrepreneurial retailer looking to grow and scale their business. As our sector goes through seismic change it is essential that every retailer understands and implements the basics that underpin every retail business. The five pillars in this book spell that out clearly.

Richard Lim – CEO of Retail Economics and retail commentator

A wonderfully insightful read. Richard's depth of experience in the retail market inevitably means he has many nuggets to share with aspiring individuals and businesses alike. The book manages to pull out the many interwoven strands of retail into succinct, tangible parts, which can then be applied to any number of retail models. Become A Retail Pioneer is both encouraging and hopeful, making a very strong case that not only is retail very much alive, it can be thriving for the savvy independent retailer.

Tom Wilson – Founder of Curio Studio

Richard, you've captured a selfless guide for others that may wish to be business entrepreneurs from your experiences in own and corporate shopkeeping world. Setting up a business is a bit like snakes and ladders and having someone who's been there like you really helps others see the coming ups from the downs. I like the way you prompt the reader to look out for 'friend or foe' and ask questions of the journey so far, who you should take with you and others to swerve clear of. I can also see your smile in your writing that helps the reader know that there's the ultimate thrill in this for them if they get it right and to reassure them if they fail a few times to then laugh it off and have another go.

Ian Shaw – Retail Director Moss Bros

I read this book and found myself agreeing out loud with Richard! He's perfectly captured the essence of a successful customer-facing business. The five pillars of retail that make up the Retail 360 methodology are the bedrock you should build your business on. Enjoy reading this book!

Richard Woods – Founder of the Lead Gen Academy and finalist on The Apprentice

I wish I had read this book before I started Pure. It is spot on. Follow every tactic; the insights are clear, informative, and inspirational and will transform your retail business.

Spencer Craig – Founder of Pure

BECOME A

RETAIL PIONEER

THE FIVE-PILLAR METHODOLOGY THAT WILL TAKE YOU FROM SHOP OWNER TO BRAND OWNER

RICHARD CROSS

DEDICATION

For Sam, Harry, and Ollie. My world.

CONTENTS

INTRODUCTION

THE MEDIA IS WRONG

Ignore the headlines, retail is not dead. It is however going through seismic changes.

To keep up is harder than ever. Increasingly retailers, both large and small, are going bust or facing up to the reality that they will have to close their stores.

It's hard.

Needing to keep cash coming in, managing staff who don't sell enough, and ensuring customers are walking through the door is the day-to-day reality for small and medium sized retail business owners.

Retail, like all old and established industries, has been through change many times before. There have always been new trends emerging, new ways of selling, and new ways of reaching a broader spectrum of customers.

What has never changed is that the ones who do best are those who understand their customers and strive every day to meet their customers' wants and needs.

THE THREE BIGGEST CHALLENGES FACING INDEPENDENT RETAIL

In every town, on every high street, both online and in offline stores, there are countless examples of retail businesses thriving. You probably know who they are near you.

It all seems so effortless. Customers walk in and carrier bags walk out.

Yet, in most retail businesses the opposite is true.

When I survey retailers and listen to the challenges they face, it always boils down to three clear things:

- **I'm constantly worried about cash flow**
- **I don't have enough customers**
- **My sales people are not good enough**

This book will provide you with a multitude of tactics and a winning strategy to address these three challenges.

WHAT IS AN INDEPENDENT RETAILER?

Independent retailers are the lifeblood of the economy. They provide jobs, a service, and communities big and small need them now more than ever.

For the purpose of this book, I assume an independent retailer to have between two and twelve shops. Not one. You can't have one

4

anymore. You must have at least two, together with an online store to complement your physical store. You must meet your customers where they are, or you will fail. You will fail because there are others who will steal your customers if you are not trading where your customers are. Why would you work hard to acquire a new customer in your shop only to see them taken by someone else in the digital sphere? It's madness. There are no excuses for not being online anymore. Don't worry if that scares you, I will show you how.

If you grow beyond 12 stores, things will look different from the business you had before. More things are decided by head office and the true connection to each of your customers will be strained. Worst of all, there are probably investors looking for additional returns on their cash. Good luck. You may find yourself looking back longingly at the days when you were smaller.

THE PIONEERS

This book is written with a specific audience in mind. It is for the changemakers, the passionate, the independent retailers with a dream, an ambition, and a determination to share their skills, hobbies, and service with the communities where they choose to do business. This book is for retail pioneers.

I truly believe retail has never been so exciting. This book is to encourage you to keep going undaunted. I will not say your past has been a mistake, or you should have done it differently. No. Your journey has been critical in bringing you to where you are now.

This book is not written for large high street brands. If that's you then a big welcome to you. You will find plenty of useful tips in here but forgive me if I tailor my thinking to the independent retailers.

This book is for those who are totally committed to making money. To making a permanently viable and profitable business. For those who absolutely want to build an incredible brand with outstanding customer service.

THERE ARE NO QUICK WINS

Don't read on if you are looking for advice on daily opening and closing checklists, or guidance on rotas or cashing up. I'm not going to cover it here; you would be far better off going and working part-time for a big high street brand and learning from them. Generally, the day-to-day store operations training is brilliant.

There are no quick wins or silver bullets in this book, and I won't deny that it's going to be hard. But there are plenty of gems that, when intertwined around the five pillars of retail, will create a self-fulfilling strategy for success and profit. You will need to continuously revisit your strategy and update it, but by the end of the book and the start of putting the practices into place you will be hooked on that anyhow.

The methods in this book will give you a plan that you can implement in an affordable and achievable way. A plan that all your team can buy into with confidence.

This book explains in detail the five pillars of retail that make up the Retail 360 methodology which I have created. It gives you the tools to understand and then implement a strategy across Customer, Brand, Product, People, and Sales. This methodology will keep your customers coming back more often, spending more money and will ensure that your brilliant sales staff won't want to leave.

Following the five pillars of retail that make up the Retail 360 methodology will enhance your business. It will let you enjoy yourself more at work, and with these strategies in place, it will also give you the freedom to spend more time outside of your work.

PART 1

THE CHALLENGE FACING RETAIL TODAY

PASSION ISN'T ENOUGH

A few years ago, I met a lady running a cake decorating business. For 25 years she had been a nurse in an NHS hospital and always brought in the best cakes. Everyone said she should open a cake shop. Finally, she followed her dream and launched her first store.

When we were introduced, she was lost. She knew lots about cakes and cake decorating but very little about retail.

Her business was taking only a small amount of money, her health was suffering, she was working every hour in the week, and she could not see how to break this cycle.

I worked with another couple of ladies who owned an independent fashion business. They had three stores and had built a good community of regular, loyal shoppers. They had started out in retail with a deep-rooted love affair for fashion. They'd enjoyed touring the vintage shops and boutique fashion brands in the back streets of Islington in London, and decided that they should open their own shops where they lived. However, their staff were a continuous headache.

At the heart of every independent retailer's business there is a passion for the product they sell. Wine and gin connoisseurs are found in off licences. Foodies in butchers. Cake decorators in bakers. I know a cheese-loving policeman who gave it all up and started the best cheese shop in Hertfordshire.

Sadly, for most retailers, they end up resenting their passion. Rather than cooking or making clothes they are worrying about payroll, sales, and underperforming staff.

BUSINESS SENSE

I am often introduced to someone who is thinking of opening a shop. I always start by asking them why. After a couple of minutes of listening to their ideas, which almost always relate to their passion, I interrupt and ask them how much money they want to make.

'What would you be comfortable with paying yourself? £20,000 a year? Doesn't seem much after working 50–60 hours a week, including every weekend for the first three years does it?'

'How about £50,000 a year?' That tends to be the lower end of acceptability to most of them.

I then set about explaining profit and margin. Most retailers have a profit margin after tax of around 4–6%. The good ones might be around 10%. Some of the best food and beverage retailers might make up to 12%–15%. More than that? No.

12

So, now I break it to them. They will be a few years off becoming a great retailer. To take home their £50,000 they will need to be doing at least £500,000 a year in sales and they will need to be a full-time employee of that business. 'How many of your products will you need to sell to hit £500,000?' I ask. Often their faces turn gloomy. It's not that I want to burst their bubble. I really don't. Retail needs the passionate. I just want to save them years of heartache and stress on their families.

If you're in the game of independent retail, you must be prepared to go the distance.

You will need two passions: one, your product, the other, growing your business. The second is much, much more important.

SELLING OUT AND CASHING IN

I once tried to buy a men's business wear retailer that operated at the lower end of the value spectrum. They had some brilliant brands at low prices. I was attracted by the great store locations, the absence of a website and there was no merchandising system in place. I could see so much low hanging fruit that with a few changes would quickly drive increased profits into the business. The business sale failed because we couldn't agree on a fair valuation of the business.

If you think you are going to become rich selling your business, you need to spend every day building that business so that it's worthwhile someone parting with their cash for the value you want to achieve. Simply ask yourself what you would pay to buy your business today. The first offer won't be as much as that.

RETAIL CLOSURES

Anyone observing retail right now will tell you the situation is dire. Store closure rates appear to be rocketing. The media is hooked on the slow death of the high street story. Big household brands are failing every month. Hundreds, sometimes thousands of brilliant, dedicated team members find themselves out of a job. It can be devastating to watch.

So, why does this seem to be worse now than ever before? It's not just one thing. You can't blame the internet or the upward only rents or the business rates on their own. It's all those things combined and much more.

Since the financial crash of 2008, we have seen historically low interest rates. It's good for borrowers but it's not good for investors who want to make returns on cash. High streets and shopping centres are majority-owned by institutional landlords often backed by pension funds.

Big corporate businesses demand an above inflation return on investment. They must keep hiking up rents, hence upwards only rent reviews, to ensure the value of their property portfolios continues to grow. The value of the business or pension fund is linked to the property value. If the properties are empty or if the rents don't grow above inflation, then the value of the business will be seen to be declining and big corporations and their investors will not stand for that.

It's a proverbial pack of cards. If the rent doesn't come in or the rent doesn't go up, so the property value declines and the whole thing falls over.

Business rates are linked to rentable value. As rents rise, so do rates. Can you see why neither the government nor the big pension fund-backed landlords want rents to go down?

Moving away from property, costs are going up everywhere. In the UK we have seen the adoption of the Living Wage which is higher than the national minimum wage. Globally, oil prices are increasing which affects the costs of goods all over the supply chain. If your currency is performing badly against the dollar, as the pound has been for the last decade, then everything just costs more.

Political uncertainty, such as the Brexit debate that gridlocked the UK from 2016–2020, creates currency devaluation and the lack of political clarity breeds uncertainty and frustration which then generates concern and further belt tightening by the consumer.

When you look at the macro factors above, it's amazing anyone has made any money over the last few years. But that's not all.

Of course, there is then the influence of e-commerce. More and more retail sales are moving online. While the pure online retailers don't have the rent and rate challenges, don't be misled into thinking it's all easy for them. Ask an online retailer the cost and impact of returns and cost per acquisition of a customer on their business and you will realise it's not all roses on the internet either.

There is huge oversupply in the retail market both online and in-store, so a natural 'check' is taking place. There are simply too many fashion stores and restaurants and coffee shops. Whatever the sector there is far too much. As the Global CEO of a FTSE 250 retailer told me in 2019, 'There will be a rationalisation of the high street. There has to be.' The closures of so many premises we saw in the wake of the coronavirus outbreak was in fact being forced by multiple factors; a number of premises had been clinging on to survival for a while.

POUND OF FLESH

Many larger retail businesses are no longer owned by the founders. Private equity (PE) houses have people trained to look for new opportunities. If they see a brand that is showing continuous sales growth, increasing profits, and a large following on social media then they will start sniffing around to see if they can jump on board.

Successful brands are quickly snapped up by investors who offer the founders a chance to take some money home for the first time in many years. Finally, the owner who has spent many years and hours building a brand can take the holidays they dreamt of and buy the house they've always wanted to live in. Why wouldn't they do that?

PE houses only want one thing. Money. The only thing that motivates them is seeing the money that they have invested grow, and grow fast. Typically, the PE house is looking for an exit three years after they bought in. The winners in this game are those that spotted the right brand and opportunities and bought in at the first stage. The first PE house that owns your brand will be the good guys. The business will do great things under their stewardship. The founders remain on board, innovating, expanding and everything they touch works.

Sure, there is a cash bonus for the founders if everything goes well, but that's not why they are doing it. The PE house will have brought in some superb skills and talent that the business could only have dreamt of before, allowing the brand to do even more remarkable things.

After three years it's time for the PE house to exit, so they go and source another PE house and show them how much money they've made. The new PE house has been circling for a while and, eager to jump on the money train, they pay an inflated valuation based on the previous year's profits. The first PE house heads off to their next venture with buckets of cash and a case study of success to woo the founders of another innovative brand. The new PE house now needs to see a return on its investment. And they look at everything.

They cut costs where they can. The regional manager who had 10 stores now has 20 stores to care for. The design department is restructured around a new consolidated model. No one involved quite understands what these words mean but what is clear is that there are now fewer people doing more work.

In a bid to grow sales, stores are opened in towns where previously the brand would never have considered opening. Prime locations are sought, and upfront cash premiums paid to secure expensive leases.

Slowly the brand is no longer the darling of its tribe of followers. It was cool to buy their products when only a handful of people knew about it. Now everyone has it, the cool people are moving on to the next thing.

Sales start to decline and the impact of the high property costs kick in. In come the expensive external advisors to sort it out and inevitably the best talent in the business moves on.

An eye watering example of this is the acquisitions of the lifestyle clothing brand Fat Face in the 2000s.

In 2000 the founders sold 40% of the company to PE house Livingbridge for £5 million. In 2005 Advent International, a PE company, bought Livingbridge's interest in Fat Face in a deal valuing the company at circa £120 million. Less than two years later, in 2007, Fat Face was acquired for £360 million by PE group Bridgepoint Capital. The business was very highly leveraged when the financial crash hit in 2008 and it took another four years before the business finally returned to a small profit in 2012.

Is it any wonder that stores start closing? In the last 20 years there was a glut of store openings. Brands awash with cash expanded and expanded some more. PE was determined to see a return on investment and so the massive oversupply of stores we see today emerged. Supply then outweighs demand.

EXPERIENTIAL RETAIL

Those close to retail now will be aware of the rising demand for experiences. People want fewer 'things' but more experiences. Richard Lim, CEO of Retail Economics, talks of "Creating meaningful experiences". This is where the consumer is moving to right now and the pressure is on the retailer to deliver it. That will be far easier offline than online.

Experiential is good and important to consider, but experiencing engaged, great service while buying a product is still more important than any experiential gimmick. Don't trip yourself up trying to over-deliver it. For most people, the following will always be the case: people want to own; people want to consume; people want to buy. Nothing gives an instant endorphin kick than buying a great product. Retail must succeed in stimulating those happiness hormones. The experience that goes with the purchase ensures your customers will come again and tell their friends all about it.

CVAs

I'm not a fan of CVAs (company voluntary arrangements) – a procedure whereby companies can reduce their debts. It also allows a struggling business to restructure its estate. This means it can close underperforming stores, negotiate rent reductions with its landlords, restructure its debts and make alterations to its management team while continuing to trade – and I do wonder if the government will tighten the rules on them. Insolvency practitioners will tell you that a CVA should only be considered if there is a genuine chance the business can be saved and will be better off by removing a few onerous leases. Fundamentally the business must be a viable going concern for the CVA to be warranted.

It does seem as though there are a few too many companies trying CVAs because they just want to be rid of some bad deals they have done.

NOT ENOUGH TALENT

I'm often surprised by bigger companies when a new finance director is brought in who has never worked in retail before. Sure enough they strip back where they can and cut costs in areas that while they don't show a financial return were the priceless elements that appealed to customers. The financial principles are the same as other businesses, but the new FD just lacks experience of the problems and opportunities these businesses are facing.

I love cheese and for a birthday present my wife bought me a cheese making course. A great experiential gift. In the week prior to my course, the executive team of a well-known cheese brand had attended. They were HR, finance, retail experts with no idea how to make their own product. It's fascinating, and yet no surprise when mistakes in strategy creep in.

Top to bottom there is not enough skill and certainly not enough training. It's a tragedy that the graduate programmes at Marks and Spencer and John Lewis and Partners have been halted. Some of the greatest leaders – not just in retail – started out in these programmes. They were given a breadth of experience in multiple functions before choosing the best career path for them. It reaped rewards and when you look at these businesses struggling today, you can't help but wonder whether they should have kept these programmes going.

I started the book by saying the media was wrong, that retail was not dead. Having read this chapter, you will be inclined to think the media is right. Always remember that the media needs to sell newspapers and fill airtime and to win more readers and viewers so they can sell advertising space. It's a far more readable story to say there are losses, redundancies, and bankruptcies. We're all quick to scoff and reflect on what each brand was doing wrong.

But, the core reason each one of these retailers failed is they failed to adapt. They failed to recognise what was happening right in front of them, and the one thing that makes retail so very exciting right now. Retail is changing.

EMERGING TRENDS

We live in an age of consumerism. In a consumer-led world everything is about convenience and choice. Retailers are expected to deliver this in a personal and experiential way.

There is a small but perceptible backlash against the world of consumerism. With greater understanding of supply chain and sustainability, Generation Z are increasingly aware of the environment and their impact on it. I asked some food influencers what trends they were seeing coming through and they all agreed it was sustainability.

Foodies care about the provenance of the product they are eating. They don't want mozzarella from Italy when they are in the south east of England, they want mozzarella from a buffalo grazing in a field 15 miles away. Why repeatedly import the mozzarella when you can import the buffalo?

It sounds counter intuitive, but consumerism and sustainability will have to become happy bedfellows. Your customers will keep on shopping. There will always be an insatiable appetite to buy and own new and better things. Just keep an eye on your supply chain and make sure it's something you would be proud to tell your granny about. Everyone in the chain needs to be paid a fair wage and your impact on the environment should be minimised continually. Fortunately, this is becoming easier to do.

More and more frequently you will see messages on menus saying £1 from this item goes to a charity or an NGO that is aligned with that firm's mission, culture or values. Shoppers will demand to know where products were made, where food was grown, what conditions are like for workers in a factory. Retailers will need to know the answers to these questions. Some will tell their customers about it upfront.

Consider this. If a luxury brand puts an extra £500 on a £5000 handbag, this will not change their business model, it definitely will not change the usefulness of the handbag or probably the decision to buy the handbag, but that £500 could be spent on a child's education in Africa.

You need to align good intentions with good execution in the 2020s. Be kind.

Giving generously is not solely about corporate social responsibility, it's about competitive advantage. And that is a good thing. Done well you will win as a retailer and the beneficiaries of your giving will win from your well executed intentions.

The failure of many stores is leading to a changing rent structure. Increasingly retailers can negotiate a performance-related rent based on a concession fee. For example, 15% of your net sales goes to the landlord as rent. The better you do the better the landlord does.

Smart retailers are working out how to trade all day. If you're paying rent for a building 24 hours a day, why is it only open for 1/3 of that? In travel locations and large shopping centres where concession fee rents are the norm, retailers are continually asking themselves how they can take more money in each hour of the day. "What is my strategy at 4am, 8am, 3pm, 8pm?"

THE FUTURE OF THE HIGH STREET

Many years ago, the high street sprung up around core services like doctors' surgeries, pharmacies, hairdressers, dentists, schools, and banks. The retailers cottoned on and opened stores there. Butchers, bakers, and the like moved out of their market stores and into buildings. Slowly the markets went away and eventually rents went up, supermarkets moved in and the core businesses moved out.

If the government is truly determined to rescue the high street, then these core footfall drivers need to be brought back into the centre. There needs to be fewer shops. Those that are there need to be experts in their sector. Business rates need to be dropped to ensure that the core businesses and retailers can afford to do brilliant things well.

Thankfully, it does seem as though change is finally coming. For you to succeed you must not worry about these things. They are out of your control. You need to focus on being brilliant at what you do. It's going to be a roller coaster, but these are exciting times for retail and the best independent retailers are about to become highly successful.

SUMMARY

This combination of fast rising costs, the explosion of online, and the demand for experiences is causing the impacts on the high street we see today.

For many retailers their mindset is in a terrible place. If you believe you will fail you will only see the signposts around you that tell you everything is looking bleak and eventually failure is your only solution.

When your business is in a downward cycle you need to step out of the storm and look at it proactively and dispassionately. Make the necessary changes before it's too late.

OUR SURVEY TOLD US

During my career I have looked after the retail estates of a large British airport business. This brought me access to CEOs, MDs, and business development directors of some of the most iconic names in British retail. I would never miss the opportunity to pick their brains on retail, the challenges they faced, and the solutions they had come up with, and I was privileged to hear their responses. I wanted to know what trends were emerging, how sales were going. How was the performance of their newest store? Where were they opening next?

As well as working in large businesses, my first love is small businesses and it's where I started out. The agility, enthusiasm, and attitude of entrepreneurs is infectious, and I can spend hours chatting with retail pioneers about new products and new opportunities. Large corporates are different, but the buzz is still there. Within a large corporate there will be many smaller departments. Often these are businesses within businesses.

If you've worked in a large business, you will know that boards and leaders love to have a strategic plan. There is a plan for this year, the three year plan, the five year plan and for large infrastructure businesses you might hear about the 25-year plan. The plan is what they use to go and ask the business for funding to invest. It is also designed to hold them to account. 'You said you would do this by this date. How have you performed?'

With bonuses and pay reviews on the line, it's the document that measures success.

Every business needs a plan. Every business needs targets. Every business needs key performance indicators. The more you have, the better you will do. In the Sales pillar in Part 2, I talk about one of my favourite mantras: "Everything measured, improves." Large businesses live by this.

THE BIG THREE PROBLEMS FACING RETAILERS

I started consulting and advising independent retailers in 2011 whilst setting up a casual lifestyle clothing brand. Very quickly I found that I loved meeting with these brands. Their budgets varied dramatically but they were unified in their ambitions and dreams to grow their businesses.

I started my retail consulting business to keep income coming in whilst I raised the finance to launch the clothing business, however it quickly became a business in its own right. I soon became a regular keynote speaker at the British Business Show. At one point I was flown to Oman to meet with princes, foreign ambassadors, and football leaders and sit in the VVIP box for a crucial football World Cup qualifier.

Surveying independent retailers to understand where their business is at is a crucial tool for my consulting business. It gives us a feel of the problems they are facing and the opportunities they have realised in their business. When all the results are combined it draws a clear picture of the health of independent retail in the UK.

Some things have emerged since I did my first surveys, such as the impact of social media as a selling tool. Others haven't changed. My purpose in doing the surveys is to ensure that the training and consultancy we can offer our clients is tailored to the needs and wants of the business owner.

The findings boil down to three key factors:

- **I'm constantly worried about cash flow**
- **I don't have enough customers**
- **My sales staff are not good enough**

The order can change for some; but generally, the priority is as they are listed above.

My experience of meeting with multiple retail brands, big and small, is that it is clear the best businesses have a plan for these big three problems. The big three problems won't go away, so highly successful businesses have acknowledged them and dealt with them head on. They dedicate time and energy to the whole package that makes up their business to ensure that customers already want to walk through their doors, to ensure the customers will spend money when they do so, and to ensure their brilliant people are ready to help each customer spend as much money as possible.

You're reading this book because you want to grow your business. Perhaps you have a highly successful retail business already and are looking to step up to the next level. Maybe you are struggling with just one of the three big problems; many of the readers of this book will be struggling with all three.

FACE INTO THE CHALLENGE

There are few things more miserable than an empty shop. I can't stand it as a retailer. I can't stand it as a customer. Every day, at every hour you need to be striving to ensure there are customers in your shop and that your people are ready to take as much money off them as possible. Nothing else matters.

If there is a quiet day in your week then plan for it to be busy next week. Caffè Nero did this. They could see that the quietest part of their week was Tuesday afternoons, so they introduced 'Free Coffee Tuesday'. One per week per customer. It was a corporate partnership with 02 that benefitted both businesses.

OK, ATV (average transaction value) was down, but footfall and therefore transactions and store penetration (some retailers refer to conversion rather than penetration; I cover this in the final chapter of Part 1: "The Science of Retail") was significantly up and that's a good thing. Once you have customers in your store, you can go to work on driving sales.

You don't need to partner with a major telecommunications business. Any independent coffee shop owner could just advertise it to their customers when they come in for a morning coffee. They could plaster it over their social media accounts with an hourly countdown to it starting.

But what if you did partner with a complementary but non-competitive business. Someone who shares the same customers as you but not the same market. How about a local gym? All their members can have free coffee in your store on Tuesday afternoons.

Suddenly you have a whole new band of customers coming in during the quietest time of your week. The gym should pay you something towards it as well.

Doing surveys and meeting retailers has given me a clear insight into the state of retail in the UK. There are those doing a phenomenal job. There are far more who are not. By nature of the fact you have picked up this book you are in the minority who genuinely want to make real change to their businesses.

If you truly want to make more money for yourself, want to spend less time in your stores, and less time worrying about the big three problems, then you need to start acknowledging them and dealing with them. Countless retailers spend time blaming outside influences on their business. We regularly hear the following gripes:

- **Parking charges in town have gone up**
- **The new one way system is a nightmare**
- **Footfall is down**
- **Shops are shutting in my town**
- **The internet is taking away customers**
- **Rents are going up**
- **Business rates are going up**
- **Retail is dead – it's all doom and gloom**

If you can genuinely control any of these things then go for it, but the chances are you would be better off facing into the things that your business can look after.

EXIT STRATEGIES

All too often I meet people who want out. They have had enough. The passion that attracted them to the business in the first place has disappeared. It is so sad to see. When I ask people how they feel about their business I frequently hear them say:

- **I want to sell my business**
- **I've fallen out of love with my business**
- **I want to spend more time outside my business**

Let's take each one of these in turn.

I WANT TO SELL MY BUSINESS

If your motivations for selling your business are based on it not working as you hoped, you have low or no profits, and you have to spend every spare hour running a shop, then no one is going to want to buy your business. You probably earn less than the minimum wage and if someone does want to buy it why would they want to swap their life for yours? On average retail businesses are sold for approximately two times their annual profits. If you are offered this valuation and your business is as I've described in this paragraph, then take their money. You will not have a better offer. The truth is very few people buy unprofitable businesses. You need to turn it around.

I'VE FALLEN OUT OF LOVE WITH MY BUSINESS

This is the saddest of them all. The great intentions at the outset when you planned the store and opened it to huge fanfare seem so far away. Your friends and family patting you on the back for saying you were going to do something and actually doing it. Not many people do that, and you did. Well done for following that dream. Was it worth it? Hell yeah! Don't regret the journey, regret the outcome. Think what you have learned. But first, before you walk away, can we reignite that passion? Is it extinct or just dormant? This book will give you the tools to achieve those dreams. You need to turn it around.

I WANT TO SPEND MORE TIME OUTSIDE OF MY BUSINESS

This is crucial, and I suggest you start today. Take tomorrow off. Take next week off. Book two weeks off in six weeks' time. Step away from it. You need head space to plan and strategize. To read books like this and allow yourself time to pause, digest, think, consider, and reflect. I know I do my best thinking lying in the sun on a beach miles away from it all. I feel the heat of the sun go through me. If I can't go to a beach I exercise. It produces the same effect. Endorphins are released. When I'm fully relaxed, I can finally start to address the challenges. Somehow, they are nowhere near as challenging as they seemed. Make a strategy, address the problems. If you execute the strategy you will have your own people running the different parts of your business. In time they will require you to spend less time working in the business and more time strategizing. You owe it to them to do so. You owe it to your people to spend less time in your business. To do this, you need to turn it around.

For you, from now on it's not about retail, it's about mindset. You need to be determined not just to follow your passion but to grow your business.

RETAIL HAS NEVER BEEN SO EXCITING

Good news is coming. The next decade will be revolutionary for retail. Massive change has been underway for a while and that is a good thing. While many household brand names have and will continue to disappear, new ones will emerge that become an ever-present part of our lives.

Look at the pace of change since the turn of the millennium with the growth of the internet and mobile devices. Look at what happened in the 2010s. Facebook, Twitter, WhatsApp, LinkedIn, Instagram mean we can learn, share, and communicate instantly with anyone anywhere. We can follow the thoughts and exploits of industry leaders in a boardroom and teenagers in a bedroom. Everyone has a voice. It has never been easier to find and connect with your customers.

THE OPPORTUNITIES AND TECHNOLOGIES ARE AVAILABLE, AFFORDABLE, SIMPLE TO USE, AND SIT IN THE PALM OF YOUR HAND

The opportunities that are available to all of us have never been greater. What was previously created by big brands in design departments, media departments, PR departments, and marketing departments can now be produced by all of us, quickly and affordably. It's not hard, the tech innovators strive continuously to make their products user-friendly. They know their customers don't have time to learn and write code, so they make it simple for you to adopt their product.

The technological advancements in the space of media alone mean that everyone can have their own TV channel on YouTube. You can produce and edit your own videos yourself or for very little money outsource it to someone else. You can add music and subtitles from your phone while sitting in bed. Making brochures and printing them has never been easier. The formats are pre-designed and there are hundreds to choose from. You can choose from designers scattered all over the world to design your logo or graphic for very little cost and have it back to you in a few hours. For free you can hold the database of all your customers in one place, set up a multi-week communication plan at the touch of a button and only need to do it once. You can create a group on Facebook dedicated to your engaged, local customers. You can source products from all over the world without having to buy a plane ticket. You can speak to your suppliers face to face at any moment.

Both the clothing businesses I have built and run have been made up almost entirely of our own brand and range of men's and women's clothing. I've seen how much easier it has become to design, source, and manufacture your own stock over the last 10–15 years. Previously, we would have to climb on a plane to the far side of the world and hand over designs and samples and wait weeks for them to come back. Now every step of the process can be done remotely. The margins you make on your own brand are at least double what you will make buying from a supplier. And, if you want, you can then sell your design to others, become the supplier yourself, create a wholesale and distribution business that will make your order quantities bigger. This will drive down your product costs and increase your margins.

PROPERTY OPPORTUNITIES

I mentioned earlier that there is oversupply on the high street and that there needs to be a natural check on the number of retailers out there. Don't be put off by this. It doesn't need to include you. The risk is considerably greater for the bigger brands. They have huge head office overheads of people, systems, travel budgets, office, and warehouse property costs etc. Their stores are in premium locations, often with rent deals done at the top of the market when their brand was soaring high. Many of them have lost touch with the needs and wants of their customers as they have tried to grow faster and faster to meet the needs of investors.

This is great news for the independent retailer. With the media full of stories of store closures and an increase in empty shops, landlords are tripping over themselves to do deals and fill stores. Landlords still have mortgages to pay and business rates to pay on an empty property.

Negotiating with landlords is easier than ever; the retailer holds the power now and you should keep pushing them down and playing one off against another until you have the best possible deal. Once you're there, go and ask for a bit more. You'll be amazed what you can achieve when the other side thinks the deal is done. In negotiating, nothing is agreed until everything is agreed. Keep nibbling away. I will dive deeper into negotiation skills in Part 2.

Fortunately, times are changing and landlords would prefer their properties are let rather than paying business rates on empty properties. The wise ones take a pragmatic view. Now more than ever deals can be done. Some of the good institutional landlords will take the approach that they would rather be 70–80% let with income coming in and the property being maintained than 50% let and bills coming in. Shopping centres and malls are doing deals on rents to avoid having empty retail units.

One thing to be wary of is smaller independent landlords who may only have one, two or three properties. Imagine the latter; with one empty they are only 66% let and then they try and chase the big rents to shore up their income. Always check how many properties a landlord has when you are negotiating. It might help you understand their motivations.

BUSINESS RATES

The UK government earns a huge amount of tax from business rates so it's no surprise that they are in no rush to change it. Fortunately, the message has landed, and they know that this cash cow has been milked dry. It's contributing to the decline of the high street and frankly it is out of date.

In 2020 the UK government finally announced business rates relief for the smaller retailers with annual rents below £51,000. This archaic system needs to be replaced with a performance-related tax akin to VAT. It's insane that a small independent retailer with a fraction of the sales potential is paying the same rates as a national chain in an identical shop next door.

This tax will change, and the winners will be the small businesses and the independent retailers like you.

STARTING UP

You can start up a retail business far cheaper than before. It used to be scruffy and a bit East End rag trade to open in a market. Now markets are becoming cool and hyper trendy. Places like Box Park have low entry, short-term leases available in multiple locations. Their retail units are old containers. Street food brands can try out in small locations with a captive audience at venues like Kerb or at a farmers' market in a church hall for a tiny amount of upfront cash.

It's a far better way to test your product idea with a captive audience than to commit to a long-term lease on a property.

LOCAL INDEPENDENTS ARE EXPERTS – THEY BREED TRUST AND THEY ARE GROWING

Business researchers have found plenty to bring us hope. The number of independent outlets has risen all over England in every region. Contrast this with the high street brands' continuing decline. Jessica Moulton at Mckinsey & Company provides some useful insights. Millennials are 3.7 times more likely to avoid buying from major consumer companies. They are 2.8 times more likely to believe newer brands are more innovative and 2.5 times more likely to buy from an independent.

Shoppers are realising that they want a more enjoyable, sustainable shopping experience. They want to be valued as a customer spending money. They enjoy being recognised. We like chatting to the butcher about how to cook something or what to try next week. Have you tried doing this in a supermarket? Often the person behind the meat counter has not been trained in how best to use their product. This is where the independent retailer can clean up.

You are without question the expert; no one knows their product as well as an independent retailer. It's one area where the big high street chains cannot compete with you. They will never be able to inspire all their people about the subtleties and nuances of your product as an expert like you can. You are convenient to all your local shoppers. As the mood moves away from the big stores, the local independents can step in and provide a far better shopping experience. One that in many instances commands a premium price for a superior product.

EMERGING FROM CORONAVIRUS

I was writing this book during the lockdown for coronavirus in the spring of 2020. Throughout this period, I was watching to see how retail would emerge from the crisis.

One rule I adopted in my writing was to ensure that everything in this book is timeless. If there is a tactic or strategy here, then it will work for the next decade or more. Some of the big changes that will come with 5G, voice recognition, AI, and newer technologies that we haven't heard of yet, will take a while to affordably filter down to independent retail.

However, free and affordable evolutions, such as shopping by social media, will become normal. Whatever the developments, I can be certain that the five pillars of Customer, Brand, Product, People, and Sales will be as important in the future as they are today.

What was clear while we saw the impact of the pandemic spread across the globe was that there was going to be so much pain for business and that the biggest businesses would suffer the most. My heart went out to the brilliant retail employees who found themselves out of work.

However, it was also a time where I was becoming excited for the opportunities that the crisis would bring and particularly those opportunities that the pandemic would present to the independent retailers who would benefit from being smaller and much more agile. The number of retailers in the market was contracting, the much-needed check on oversupply on the high street was taking place.

"From a brand perspective, there is an opportunity for retailer brands to achieve their holy grail; a genuine emotional connection with their customers. Brands that create hope and reassurance during uncertain times will certainly be held closer than those who appear uncaring or worse profiteering in their communications."

Kathryn Middleton, Director, Proper Marketing

Change was coming in retail; the pandemic accelerated that change far quicker than anything else could have. Overnight we have found new ways of shopping and communicating because we were forced to. Old habits have changed rapidly.

SUMMARY

For independent retailers, the conditions have never been better, the future is exciting, and it's yours to grab. Retail doesn't need to be a struggle. Building a business should be great fun. There will be challenges to overcome but you know that, so enjoy the ride. Take pride from what you have already achieved, reflect on the battles you have won.

I truly believe that the next decade is going to see an explosion of independent retailers building great businesses.

I believe this because the conditions have never been better. Property costs are coming down, and consumers have more trust in smaller brands having seen through the corporate veneer of the larger chains. It's cheaper to start up than ever before. You can create branding and your own product for very little upfront cost. You can market yourself to as wide a customer base as you want. Perhaps even more powerfully, you can market yourself to as narrow and precise a customer base as you want.

What we are seeing is a set of conditions emerging that favour the smaller store. It is not just economic conditions in terms of the easing of costs, but societal trends with the emergence of a social conscience around both sustainability and giving back, aligned with the powerful reach of the internet in an affordable way, drawing customers back to the locality where they can value smaller, more specialist stores, and where they are served by experts. Times are changing and for the independent retailer it has never been so exciting.

HARNESS THE POWER OF THE DIGITAL REVOLUTION

If you're not deploying digital technologies in your business, then you need to right now. To say the future of retail is omnichannel feels outdated. It has been omnichannel for 10 years already. However, there are still a surprising number of independent retailers who are not harnessing the digital opportunity.

You need to have two stores as a minimum, one offline and one online. I truly believe this is the only way forward for all retail businesses. Even the biggest pure online retailers recognise they will need to have bricks and mortar stores in the future. Amazon already does with their Amazon Go grocery stores popping up all over the US.

When you open a bricks and mortar store you put in considerable thinking and planning to it. Sketching out the unit design, considering where the stock room will be, where the till point is, how to best display your product, and how to make best use of the windows to ensure your stock is selling all the time is key. Then you start spending the money: building the displays, fixtures and fittings, painting the walls, and adding the elements of design that are bespoke to your stores' brand image. Next you add the stock. It's now ready to open. Throughout this time people have been walking past watching and wondering what is going to open in there. Excitement is brewing. At the moment of opening you put up balloons, invite as many people as possible, perhaps give them an incentive to come to an in-store event, you thank them for coming and finally sit down, draw breath and count the cash from the first day's sales. Cash you have earned.

Now, re-read the last paragraph and instead of thinking of a bricks and mortar store, think of it as an e-commerce website.

It's critical to understand that you cannot cut corners online. The time, effort, and meticulous planning that went into your physical stores needs to go into your digital store.

Too many retailers dabble with online. They buy a cheap, maybe free, web portal sticking some product on and sending an occasional email. I don't want to knock either free or cheap e-commerce portals. There are some brilliant ones out there. I've seen one retailer turnover nearly £1 million a year on a cheap Shopify package. I was imploring them to invest in a better platform and in doing so they would have taken more money from better software and plugins. But there was no doubting how a very well managed cheap package could be powerful. The key is it was well managed. There was a brilliant dedicated employee tweaking its look and feel and managing the stock package every single day with the stores and warehouse managing the distribution.

Treat your online store like your physical store. It needs ongoing investment, time, and care. You're naïve to think you can simply build it and customers will come.

DIGITAL TECHNOLOGIES

At the start of the chapter I said you needed to be deploying digital technologies in your business. I want to pause and take a moment to explain what I mean by digital technologies. I know from talking to many retailers that there is a huge fear of the unknown associated with the words online or digital.

Remember, your fear is based on a lack of experience. It is just the unknown. The good news is, no one has a handle on every single digital advancement because there are too many to know. Even the overconfident pub bore who seems to know it all cannot possibly understand everything.

It doesn't matter that you didn't have many lessons at school in computing or IT or whatever it was called. I know I didn't, but I've still built multiple websites. You will need to be a good manager and know what your digital experience should look like for your customers, then bring in the resource to deliver it. I encourage you to give it a go or talk to a friend who can help you. As I've said already, you don't need to write code. The digital companies want you to adopt their product, so they have made it as user-friendly as possible. It is now easier than ever to build a website yourself. You will be surprised how easy it is and you will learn much more as you go.

As a minimum, the digital technologies you should be deploying are:

- **An e-commerce website – this is an online shop**
- **Regular planned email marketing campaigns**

• **Social media accounts**

Please do not be limited by this. Do what is right for your business. If it's right for you, then sell on Amazon and eBay or other marketplace websites that resonate with your brand and customers. Find multiple routes to market. Even if it only accounts for 1% of your business, it's a channel that is worth pursuing.

As soon as possible the next step that is powerful right now is video. The more of your product you can do a very short film about, the better. It only needs to be a few seconds long. You'll be astounded how many more sales you will make on products that you have brought to life with a little bit of film, subtitles, and voiceover. You can do this on your phone. You don't need to be Steven Spielberg.

Finally, start testing out advertising. I suggest you start with Google AdWords or Facebook. The key to this is testing and learning. Set small budgets, £20–£30 is plenty, and see how an advert performs. What makes this powerful is split testing. Never put one advert up. Put up two or three or six. They can all point to the same promotion but use different headlines, images or calls to action.

Then measure the results. If one of them created a greater click through rate or sales result, then ditch the rest and make more adverts like that one. You will likely be surprised what sort of messages work for your customers. Advertising can be tried, tested, and measured accurately for very little. You can set your budget and know the actual results of your investment. It's a far cry from the famous quote by John Wanamaker, considered to be a pioneer in marketing at the start of the 20th Century, "*Half the money I spend on advertising is wasted; the trouble is I don't know which half."*

Online advertising is simple to do. There are plenty of books on it although personally I'd recommend watching a lesson on YouTube. Either way, become familiar with it. It's quite addictive once you start. Keep an eye on what you are spending, start small, test various strategies, and measure the results.

We are only at the beginning of the digital revolution. This period is still relatively embryonic and will be the case for many more years as new technological solutions emerge.

Working out how to commercialise these new opportunities for your business does require you to pay attention. When the GB Cycling Team was ruling the world, winning bucket loads of medals at consecutive Olympic Games between 2008 and 2016, they were coached by the meticulously prepared Sir Dave Brailsford. Brailsford was noted for his innovative concept of 'marginal gains'. The whole principle came from the idea that if you break down everything you could think of that goes into riding a bike, and then improved it by 1%, you will have a significant increase when you put them all together. That is what I'm asking you to do with the digital revolution. You are not seeking to turn your business around overnight, but piece by piece. 1% improvement over here, 1% improvement over there. Keep looking for that marginal gain.

WHERE TO FOCUS YOUR ATTENTION

Sebastian Bates founder of Warrior Academy shared with me what he does to drive business as his only way of reaching customers is through digital means. The words below are his. The money he spends per month was right for his business in early 2020.

"I have outsourced the posts on my social media accounts (LinkedIn, Instagram, Facebook etc). It is all on auto pilot on all platforms. Then I chuck in loads of personal stuff in my own time. I also ensure all platforms are totally consistent. My cover photo and profile picture are the same for:

Facebook
Instagram
LinkedIn
YouTube
Email signature
Business cards

It builds trust, and the consistency means it's easily recognised.

To generate content, I will put aside 20 mins a week to sit down and just speak to the camera. This is edited into 10–15 videos by the team. See below.

I have outsourced the following:

Animator/Video Editor – £80 per month
Typically edits, repurposes and animates videos for me for £5–10 per video. He's a genius and can do absolutely anything I throw at

him. I ask him to use rev.com to subtitle my work at like £1 per minute because it's cheaper and more accurate than using a freelancer.

Social Media Manager – £280 per month
She does 10 hours per week and creates and schedules two posts a day (typically) and daily stories, across all platforms.

Instagram Community Manager – £250 per month
Manages our Instagram and grows it around 1,000 engaged followers per month.

Professional Photographer – £150 per month
Amazing photographer that comes in six times a year; we spread the payments over 12 months and have a constant stream of amazing photos.

Facebook Adverts Manager – £250 per month
Our adverts manager does an awesome job. I've found people who charge a fortune and who charge very little. My guy took me ages to find but does a high-quality job for a cheap price. He's also constructed an incredible mini chat bot so our customer service bill went down. We have 5–10 adverts going on all month and spend around £2–4k per month. He manages it all.

So, from this list you could pick and choose what you feel you need. These guys are very good and charge very little but I've been outsourcing for eight years to find them.

In summary, if you are super busy I'd find a social media manager and then an animator. For £350 you would have most of your stuff on auto pilot."

It's crucial that you know this is what is right for him and his business. He achieved these levels through many years of trying one resource and then ditching it or refining it. He never stood still. Like Sir Dave Brailsford he's always looking for marginal gains.

Practise setting aside an hour per week listing 10 products you wanted to promote, then create a short video about each one on your phone and send it to a video editor to tidy up and add subtitles.

They send it to your social media manager who posts it on all your social media channels at the right time and moment for your audience. This is something they should have tested and know when to do. The social media manager can also take main quotes from the videos and add appropriate pictures of the stock and post them at varying times as well.

Very quickly you will have plenty of content to go out each week.

Whatever you do online, appear to your customers as the expert. To be an expert you cannot cover multiple bases. You must niche your market to a narrow field and be the very best. Someone like Sofa.com is very clearly a market expert in the sofa niche. Not only does this help when people are searching for sofas, but it reassures the shopper that they are dealing with experts in this space.

Around your product should be heaps of information about you and your business and why you are the expert in your space. The very biggest brands cannot do this. Take advantage of their weakness and drive home your superiority.

RESOURCE

I will always encourage you to give it a go yourself. Even self-confessed technophobes have found it easier than they imagined and started leaping out of bed in the morning to see how a post has been received or how well an advert has performed.

Many years ago, youngsters were attracted to jobs in shops. They still are, but they want to work in online shops; find these digital natives and bring them into your business. Failing that, outsource it. Ask around your network or local community for recommendations and try people. Search online for someone doing what you need. Write a brief of what you want and provide them with examples of things you like.

EMAIL CAMPAIGNS

As you will have established you can't just build an e-commerce platform and wait for the money to roll in. You need to promote it.

You need an email campaign strategy for recruiting new digital customers. Going forwards, each customer should be segregated into as many subsets as possible, such as brilliant, average, occasional, and lapsed and then you create a bespoke campaign for communicating to each subset.

This may seem like hard work, however, you need to become comfortable with knowing your online shop is as hard to run as your offline shop and the strategies for both are distinct and relevant to each channel. There are plenty of CRM (customer relationship management) systems where you can create an email campaign and subset your audience. You can take advantage of free platforms, such as Mail Chimp, up to very complex, powerful tools like Salesforce or Microsoft Dynamics.

Big retailers will have teams of people just administering Salesforce and the marketing team will be tweaking and testing everything that goes out then measuring the results in intricate detail.

You don't have that resource, but you must commit to the principles. Once it is set up and you have campaigns ready to go for each of your customer groups, the sales will follow. As a minimum, commit to entering the leads and contact data as soon as it's received. Create an onboarding sequence of six to eight emails to a new customer. Welcome them and explain what sort of things they can expect to receive from you. You could invite them to an event or a personal shopping experience, maybe give things away with a first purchase.

Then create campaigns for as many subsets as you can find the time for. Consider how you are going to look after your top 1% of customers. The next 9%, the next 20%, the occasional shopper, and the lapsed. Your job is to take as much money off people as possible and make them feel good about it.

Bear in mind, your top 1% of customers could equate to 20% of income. Whatever it is for your business, spend your energy and resource appropriately to the income it will drive.

Finally, for every campaign you run, test the results. Change things based on the lessons you learned. It's very hard not to become obsessed with this once you've started. The very best will have more than one campaign for each subset of customers. Split testing again. Once they find something that works, they keep rolling it out. If a campaign fails, they ditch it straight away.

SOCIAL MEDIA

There are multiple platforms for social media. As a minimum, Facebook and Instagram must be part of your strategy. Facebook has volume. Instagram is going to be the most powerful as customers prefer watching video and short stories. Selling via Instagram and Facebook are essential sales channels that are gathering momentum. Jump on board with these platforms. The reach of social media is far bigger than you will ever achieve with the catchment area of your store. It's where your customers are spending their time, so you need to meet them there.

During the coronavirus lockdown, Facebook launched Facebook Shops. They had been working on this for a long while, but with many small businesses unable to trade, the timing for bringing this sales channel to market was excellent.

> *"Facebook Shops make it easy for businesses to set up a single online store for customers to access on both Facebook and Instagram. Creating a Facebook Shop is free and simple. Businesses can choose the products they want to feature from their catalogue and then customize the look and feel of their shop with a cover image and accent colors that showcase their brand. This means any seller, no matter their size or budget, can bring their business online and connect with customers wherever and whenever it's convenient for them.*
>
> *People can find Facebook Shops on a business' Facebook Page or Instagram profile, or discover them through stories or ads. From there, you can browse the full collection, save products you're interested in and place an order — either on the business' website or without leaving the app if the business has enabled checkout in the US."*
>
> Facebook post on the day they launched Facebook Shops.

Let's be clear, Facebook and Instagram's goals are to keep as many people as possible on their platforms so they can command greater advertising revenue. But for the small business owner it's another sign of the simplicity, both free and user-friendly, of reaching new and existing customers. You must take advantage of these evolving opportunities that make buying online easier for your customers.

Ask your customers what social media channels they are using and then meet them there.

The more you do on social media the better, not least as Google will do the rest and bump you up on to the front page of their search results. If you are new to social media then start by registering for an account and follow major brands that lead in your sector, and some that are not in your sector. Watch carefully what sort of content they are producing. Notice how often they are trying to sell a product and when they are just telling stories that help build the appeal of their brand.

DON'T WASTE TIME RESEARCHING – START AND INNOVATE AS YOU GO

Online, everyone assumes that everyone else is doing a better job than they are. They will see what one brand is doing well and aspire to be them. The truth is that we are only at the outset of the digital revolution. No one has totally perfected it, and what is right today may be out of date in a year's time.

I once sat in a breakfast seminar with the heads of social media from both Vivienne Westwood and Burberry. Both were eulogising about how good the other's brand was at social media. Both were convinced that their own work was nothing special to the complete disagreement of the other. It was a fascinating insight. The truth is that both were doing excellent things. They have different customers with different needs. What was right for Burberry's customers was not the same for Vivienne Westwood's. And vice versa. I left fully reassured that no one is totally right. What is important is that you find a way to communicate with your customers that resonates with them.

BE A GREAT IN-STORE RETAILER AND A GREAT DIGITAL RETAILER

You can't spend your time worrying about not having every digital innovation under your control. You would never keep up. If you want to reassure yourself, take a trip into the heart of British retail. Regent Street and Carnaby Street exhibit the best of the best world class brands. You won't find robots stacking the shelves, or VR (virtual reality) headsets being worn by the customers. There are some cool innovations going on in fashion stores, such as mirrors that show you in a garment, and fitting rooms that sync with your Spotify account. No one has delivered the total digital/physical solution. The very best must be the Apple store, and yet they still have well-trained staff who are fully knowledgeable about their product and dedicated to helping you understand what's best for your needs. We can all do that.

Data shows that a retail business drives 20–50% of its online sales within the catchment zone of its own stores. Consumers are more inclined to buy online from local retailers as they know it's simpler to take advantage of click and collect and to take back returns.

For this reason, John Lewis incentivise their store staff to promote their website. Each store is rewarded for how well online sales do within their defined catchment area. What John Lewis wanted to avoid was well-trained sales assistants spending hours selling to customers only to watch in frustration as they walk out and buy online. By reassuring their teams that the online sales in their area were contributing towards their own store's performance, the sales assistants could promote the website with confidence and without animosity.

Primark is a notable exception to the rule. They do not sell online. But don't be misled into thinking they are not digitally enabled. Their social media following is phenomenal. The content output on Instagram is well worth following and their social media strategies are well worth adopting. Google the videos that went with the opening of their store in Birmingham in 2019. The technological and user experience ideas that they introduced to that store are all designed to keep customers dwelling for longer. Then it's over to their great product and people to sell as much as they can.

WHAT ELSE DOES THE FUTURE HOLD?

The technology arm of locksmith Yale is working with grocery retailers in Norway and Sweden to give their delivery drivers digital key access to people's homes, allowing the driver to put the food in your fridge while you are at work. All recorded by a chest camera. When surveyed, 20% of 18–24 year olds said they would be comfortable with this access.

It's important to spot these trends. In 2020, 50% of the adult population will be Gen Zs and Millennials. This generation has grown up digitally enabled.

In their report published titled *Shaping the Future of Retail for Consumer Industries*, The World Economic Forum discusses the emerging trends of retail. From this report, they published a video on their Facebook page summarising how they predict retail will look in 2027 with eight of the biggest changes they say we can expect to see:

"*1. Sensors and digital devices will create a hyper-personalized customer experience. Customers' online activity and years of past purchase data will generate personalized suggestions.*

2. Roles not 'customer facing' – shelf stacking – will be automated. The number of jobs in retail will fall significantly.

3. Checkout will be done remotely when you leave the store with your chosen items. No more queuing or scanning your items.

4. Routine household purchases will be automatically delivered. Driverless trucks or drones will do much of the work.

5. The trend away from huge stores will continue. Customers continue to value smaller, more specialist outlets.

6. Online sales will grow from around 10% today to around 40% in 2027. In some sectors the figure will be well above 50%.

7. 3D printing will enable shops to create items on demand. This should enable many new, smaller companies to enter the market.

8. Virtual reality will change both the shop and home experience. Potential buyers will be able to browse virtual stock before buying."

ARE YOU A DIGITAL CONVERT?

The main factors driving the growth in e-commerce are price, convenience, and digital natives i.e. youngsters forming more than half the population. Digital is the default setting for this demographic and there's very little that can be done about that fact. You work hard to convert and acquire customers in your stores, and you must not let them go elsewhere online.

However, let's be clear, this doesn't mean the high street is finished, just that its nature is changing especially in relation to the e-commerce space. This is what it means to be omnichannel. Your customers will shop wherever they can. It's up to you to ensure that you can meet them where they are and that the experience they have of shopping with you is the same in each instance.

Technology has enabled small companies to work directly with people across the globe. It's never been more exciting. Digital is affordable, it is not difficult, and it is in your hands. Spend time to develop these channels. They will enhance your brand, give a better customer experience to a wider reach of customers, and bring you in more sales.

THE SCIENCE OF RETAIL

Part 1 of this book would not be complete without making sure you understand the fundamentals of retail. Apologies to those who know and understand this already. I suggest you read it through rather than skip to Part 2, if only to ensure that this is fixed in your mind.

There is a very simple equation that underpins retail. You probably know it already without having thought about it:

Transactions x ATV = Sales

TRANSACTIONS AND PENETRATION

Knowing the number of transactions you have done in a day is the bare minimum. It's far better if you measure penetration. Penetration is achieved by measuring what percentage of the customers who walked into your store made a transaction. For this you will need a footfall counter. There are many on the market and I would strongly advise making the investment. In the meantime, just keep a tally of the number of customers who walk in. If a family of four walks in, add four to your tally.

At the end of the day add up how many people walked in and add up how many transactions you made.

Total Transactions / Total Footfall = Penetration

Let's say you and I run a store. In our store today 131 people walked in and there were 47 transactions.

Total Transactions: 47 / Total Footfall: 131 = Penetration: 0.3587

Penetration rate is normally expressed as a percentage. So, multiply the penetration figure by 100.

In our store the penetration percentage rate is *35.9%.*

By the way, some retailers refer to penetration as conversion. I worked with a large restaurant group that referred to it as participation. It doesn't matter. Just choose what's right for you.

ATV

ATV is learned by totalling all the sales for the day and dividing it by the number of transactions.

Let's say today we took £1,245 in sales. This was achieved by 47 different transactions.

£1245 / 47 = £26.49

Our ATV for today is *£26.49*

So, let's apply the equation:

Transactions: 47 x ATV: £26.49 = Sales: £1,245

Retail is simple. But it is even simpler when you are completely familiar with this equation.

MAKING THE EQUATION WORK FOR YOUR BUSINESS

Whenever I'm faced with a challenge in retail, I bring it back to this equation. Equally, when I think of the three main problems our survey listed, I link it back to this fundamental equation.

If something isn't working, then either ATV needs to grow, or penetration needs to grow. Or both.

I want you to start thinking of everything you do in the context of ATV and penetration. If you grow ATV by 10% and penetration by 10%, sales go up by a huge 21%.

Our ATV was £26.49. Grow it by 10% and the new ATV is *£29.14*.

Penetration was 35.9%. Grow it by 10% and the new penetration percentage is *39.5%*.

We can calculate the number of transactions by multiplying 131 (the number of customers who walked in) by 39.5% = 51.7 transactions.

Double check the maths if you find it helps: 47 transactions + 10% = 51.7.

Now we have our new daily sales number:

Transactions: 51.7 x ATV £29.14 = Sales: £1,506.54

That's £261.54 more than the original sales total. A growth of 21%.

Can you see the power of growing ATV by 10% and penetration by 10%? In everything you do in your business, you now need to be thinking of it in terms of growing ATV and penetration.

For ATV you must be thinking how you will sell more and more to every single customer who makes a purchase.

For penetration you need to be thinking two things. Firstly, how can I attract more customers to my stores? Secondly, how can I convert more of them to buy?

Start now. Start measuring yesterday's ATV. Measure last week's ATV. Measure last month's ATV. How did they compare to the same day, week, month in the year before? Start counting your customers. Then challenge yourself to increase the penetration percentage the next day and the next day.

Very quickly these data points will become the bedrock of your business. They will be the most important tools by which you measure the health of your business.

Part 2 of this book shows you the five pillars of the Retail 360 methodology. Each pillar is built around growing ATV and penetration. Layer by layer we will break down your business into the constituent parts and then build it back up in a way that will ensure you are growing ATV and penetration.

I worked very closely with Caviar House and Prunier when I was letting space in airports. If you've ever flown through Heathrow airport you will have seen their incredible seafood and champagne bars. The company oozes premium quality at every touch point. We opened a spin off Grab and Go offer at London Stansted Airport, an airport with a predominantly low-cost airline passenger.

Very soon after it opened, I asked Suhail Rebeiz, the UK CEO, if they were pleased with it. *"Wow"* he said, *"It's the lowest ATV we have ever had, but the busiest store we've ever had."* I asked him if he was ok with this, *"Yes"* he replied. *"I would much rather have low ATV and plenty of customers. It's much easier to grow ATV than to grow customers."*

PART 2

INTRODUCTION TO RETAIL 360

Every day I am inspired by the entrepreneurs who are out there doing it. Facing challenges with a determination to make a difference in the world. This is not just the crazily successful ones whose names trip off the tongue, but equally the dedicated small business owners, the pioneers, and the creators who have come up with an idea and set about making it available and accessible for the rest of us to enjoy.

They have chosen uncertainty and risked failure to do this. Well done them.

This life is not for everyone. Some people quite rightly look at the risks and rewards and weigh that up against the success rates and conclude that on balance being an entrepreneur looks like a fool's game. I'm not going to go online now and find a statistic that tells you how good your chances of succeeding at running your own business are. I know the odds are not great. But that's not why we do it. We do it because we have a passion or we spot a gap in the market. We do it because we are inspired to do so by those who have gone before. We do it because we desperately want to make the world a better place for others. We do it because the pain of not doing it and living with regret is greater than the pain of starting the journey in the first place.

For those outside the world of entrepreneurship, the measure of success of small business owners seems to be whether you have sold your business for a mammoth return. This is so simplistic that it's infuriating.

Surely the measures of success are greater than this one binary succeed / don't succeed metric?

Is it a failure to create something all by yourself? Is it a failure to employ people every day? To be a part of the story of their lives? Is it a failure to have ordered product from suppliers who have relied on your success and your ability to pay their bills so they in turn can pay their employees and their suppliers on down the chain?

All these things, and I can go on and on, are not failures just because one day your business closed, or you had had enough, or you didn't manage to sell out for millions. Just by turning up every day and doing what you have done to start and run a business means that you are one of a very special breed who deserve every possible success. And it's not just me and your mum saying that. Every entrepreneur out there who is going through it day in and day out is rooting for you too. Keep going. You can do this.

IT WILL PAY BACK

The better your results become, the easier business will be. As your business turns over more in sales, more companies will want to work with you. You will be able to attract better suppliers and you will be able to command better fees from them to work with you.

You will attract talented people who choose to work with you over a multitude of other businesses competing to attract them.

It's often said that the first million pounds is the hardest to earn. This is going to be the case for you. The process of becoming successful is going to be hard work. You will, at times, find that things you have tried did not work as you had hoped. That the marketing you put out didn't generate a great response. That the key employee you hired turned out to be a great talker but not a great worker.

Can we accept now that this will happen? There will be road bumps. There will be days where you wished you had a regular job with a guaranteed income. Running the show, running your own business is hard yards. If you've been doing it for long enough you will have the scars and war stories to prove it. I salute you.

The next five chapters break down the Retail 360 methodology that will transport your business from the 'also-rans' to the band of successful retailers.

You personally will make more money, your business will have more customers, you will make more sales, and your staff will become your greatest asset.

The hard work will be worthwhile, and the hard work will become easier because from now on you will have a plan. There will be a rhythm to what you are striving towards and your team will buy into why you are doing it.

It will pay back.

THE RETAIL 360 METHODOLOGY TO BECOME A SUCCESSFUL RETAILER

I've said this before, and it bears repeating. *In every town, on every high street, both online and in physical stores there are countless examples of retail businesses thriving. You probably know who they are near you.*

It all seems so effortless. Customers walk in and carrier bags walk out.

When you peel back the fabric of these businesses, you will see multiple tactics being deployed. These tactics are aligned behind a handful of key strategies. The key strategies pull into one clear objective.

Alistair Campbell was for many years the spin doctor shaping the policy and creating the messages that underpinned Tony Blair and New Labour's rise to power and three overwhelming general election victories. His book, *Winners and How They Succeed* sets out three layers of building a successful team, business or in his and Blair's case a political party. These three layers are Objective, Strategy and Tactics. In the case of New Labour, the 'objective' was to overwhelmingly win the next general election. They then had a small handful of 'strategies' around areas such as messaging, key people, and policy. Behind each strategy were multiple 'tactics' that could be deployed to ensure the 'strategy' was successful and supported the 'objective' that everyone in the team was aligned behind: winning the next general election.

The Retail 360 model is built in the same way. If you don't have an objective in your business, then start with this one:

"My objective is to become a successful retailer, to create as much profit in my business as possible, so that I can do great things for my family and make a real change in the world."

The strategies you need to do this are the five pillars of the Retail 360 methodology: Customer, Brand, Product, People, and Sales. Each pillar has three parts to it.

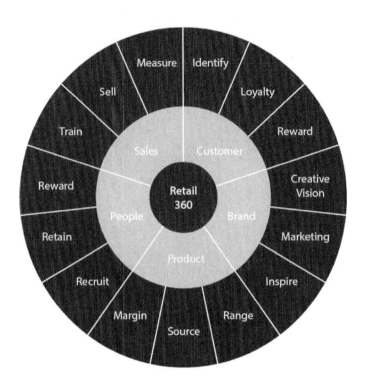

I built the Retail 360 model to show my clients the fundamentals of retail that you need to be working on every day. These five pillars and their associated parts are the most important things in your business.

Within each of the pillars I will show you multiple tactics you can deploy. Inevitably you will have tactics that you already use, and you will discover more of your own. The tactics in each of the strategies are tried and tested by the biggest and most successful retailers.

1. CUSTOMER

In retail everything starts with the Customer. You can have all the best product ideas in the world, but if no one wants to buy them you do not have a business. You need to live and breathe your customers' wants and needs.

There are three parts to the Customer pillar: Identify, Loyalty, and Reward.

2. BRAND

Once you know your Customer inside out you can build your Brand. This is not just the logo or how you appear on carrier bags or signage. This is every touch point that your customers have with you. It is also every touch point that your people and suppliers have with you. Your brand sets the tone of voice, the experience, and the expectation of what your customers, suppliers, and people will sense when they encounter your business. It is integral to every decision you take.

There are three parts to the Brand pillar: Creative Vision, Marketing, and Inspire.

3. PRODUCT

I can't tell you what product to sell. For most retailers the product they sell goes right back to their core, their reason for starting and running this business in the first place, be it a love of fashion, great coffee or an enthusiasm for meat and butchery. Product, though, is the difference between profit and loss. Product is margin. To be successful you don't just need great product, you need your product to work hard for you.

There are three parts to the Product pillar: Range, Source, and Margin.

4. PEOPLE

You can't do this on your own. And you shouldn't try to. If you do you will have a very badly paid job with none of the upside of being a business owner. There are no single person businesses that have sold out for millions. People are the most important asset you will have in your business. This is retail and it's a selling environment. You need to find the best possible people, then you need to nurture them to become superb in whatever role you have identified for them. You need to set out your expectations very clearly for that role and regularly check in to ensure those expectations are being met and exceeded. You need to help your people to be brilliant.

There are three parts to the People pillar: Recruit, Retain and Reward.

5. SALES

This shocks me every day, but whenever I ask sales assistants how much training they have had in selling it is nearly always less than till training, cashing up, dressing the window or stocking the shelves. Makes you wonder why they are called sales assistants. The base expectation of a sales assistant is that they can sell. If they have the right character, and you will have determined that through the People pillar, then with your customer identified, your brand credentials established, and your awesome product working hard for you, the sales will follow. This is guaranteed.

There are three parts to the Sales pillar: Train, Sell, and Measure.

BUILD IT LIKE THIS AND THEY WILL COME

You need to build your successful retail business in this order. It doesn't matter if you have been going for many years or if you are just starting out. Those with experience will have the benefit of hindsight, particularly when it comes to Customer and Product. But you still need to do the work. You will continuously need to do the work of examining each pillar and making sure it is fit for purpose every day.

You must start with Customer. The process you need to follow is not the process of making or buying the product and putting it on the shop floor. The process you need to follow is the process of the customer journey. You need to experience your business the way the customers do.

If you just focus on the most beautiful brand but have no customers or no sales strategy, then your business will not run cleanly and profitably. If you have the most beautiful product but your people let you down, then no one will buy it.

HAVE YOU PACKED THE FLOAT?

Whenever one of my outdoor events teams was leaving our warehouse heading out for a weekend selling clothes at one of the many sporting events we would attend each year, the last question I would ask them before the van pulled out of the yard was, "Have you packed the float?" They were going to need it.

You have worked very hard to make it this far. You are now going to have customers queuing up to do business with you. If you follow this method, and if you continuously revisit each pillar in the method then customers will be flocking to your door.

You will have built a business that doesn't need you. The parts will work because you have set the strategy, been clear about the goals and the expectations of the job, and the machine will do the rest.

My final request before you start putting these pillars into place: share this with your team. Don't go it alone. You will need to gather their insights and listen to their opinions today and tomorrow. Stay close to the Customer, stay close to the Brand, find out what People are saying about your Product, know what your People think of the jobs they are being asked to do. Then you can count the Sales and make sure the ATV is rising and the penetration is rising on an ever-growing base of customers. Don't keep this to yourself. It's much easier if everyone understands the direction of the business and where it is you are all heading.

PILLAR 1: CUSTOMER

"There are plenty of retail winners out there and lessons can be learned from many, by many. No one is going to be a winner in this market because they are good at managing costs. That has to be a given. Being great at selling is the non-negotiable skill in this market. And being good at selling has to begin and end with the customer. Investing in truly understanding your core customer, in serving them, and having the belief in your brand to not chase after peripheral business. This is what I believe is essential for retail success."

Richard Hyman, retail insights thought leader and founder of Verdict Research

Everything starts with the customer. Retail has always, and will always, start with knowing who your customer is and then giving them what they want, every time.

The Customer pillar is built around three core parts: Identify, Loyalty, and Reward.

Firstly, I will walk you through a plan of how to be crystal clear as to who your customer is. By the end you will have absolute clarity on who they are and why it is so important to be precise in your description of them.

It is a powerful process that will come very easily to some and will be harder for others. The emphasis will be on you to narrow this down and be increasingly precise about who your customer is. Once you've achieved this, many more elements of building a successful independent retail business will slot into place.

Secondly, we will look at loyalty. You've worked hard to find a customer, now you need to keep them close to you. We will explore the loyalty programmes that other brands have used, and you can see how this can be done quickly and affordably in your business. Also, we will understand why loyalty is a two-way exchange.

Thirdly, we will look at rewarding your customer which goes hand in hand with loyalty. It's not always about making sales today, it is about ensuring they won't want to go elsewhere the next time they are ready to buy.

A customer is an enormously precious asset to have. They need to be cared for and preserved forever more. You will have heard this before, but it's so true; it is far easier to make a sale to an existing customer than to a new customer. It's also the case that your existing customers are the best advert for your brand. They are going to be driving more customers into your stores than you are through any of your branding and marketing and superb product. Never underestimate the power of referrals and word of mouth. For these reasons alone you need to be looking after each one of your customers as best you can.

I attended a conference for food and drink retailers in the US where a CEO stood on stage giving the keynote speech. His career had included a long spell at Disney. His loud, repetitive mantra was this: "You need to be a maniac about customer experience." It's an outstanding rule to follow anywhere in the world.

WHO IS YOUR CUSTOMER?

When I worked at Jack Wills we had two customers: Tom and Lucy. We knew them inside out. We knew where they went to university, what sports they were playing, what drinks they were buying and in which bars they were buying them. We knew what music they were listening to, where they grew up, and we knew who they hung out with. We knew what they were doing this weekend and we knew what they did last weekend.

Of course, Tom and Lucy were not real, they were avatars. But we knew everything about them. So, when either Tom or Lucy walked into our stores, we were intuitively aware what they were interested in, what they were worried about, what their motivations were.

This may sound extreme however it was invaluable. We had team members whose job it was to go out to bars and clubs and gigs and major sporting events to meet and watch the Toms and Lucys. We wanted to know what they were doing, what they were interested in.

In different stores across the UK and eventually in the US and Middle East, Tom and Lucy would take on different forms and interests. There were local nuances that mattered to Tom and Lucy that the stores teams were tuned into. Such things as an annual music festival, the hosting of an annual sports fixture or end of year parties were common local factors that we needed to know about.

Tom and Lucy never grew up. They were always aged somewhere between 18 and 25. To stay relevant it was crucial that we knew what was important to the Toms and Lucys of today. As times change so do the customers' needs and interests. What phone are they using? What social media are they tuned into?

Can you see how important it is to stay relevant? What was right last year will not be right next year

1. IDENTIFY

The first part of the Customer pillar is to identify your customer. You need to know who is going to be buying your product. If you're a butcher in a village, is your target demographic in their twenties? No, they are going to be 40+, they are going to have jobs or partners with jobs. They are going to have pensions they live off. If you're running a coffee shop is your customer in their 60s? Or are they students or are they stay at home parents?

Ask your customers to tell you about themselves. Write surveys you can give them to fill in. Have a shortlist of questions you and your team will ask during any interaction to draw out their interests. Look at the data and spot trends. Capture the data and review it. And commit to keep on doing this. You need to be watching out for new trends in your customers' behaviour.

The restaurant chain 'wagamama' wants to hear from their customers. There is a QR code on the tables with the message "Your feedback feeds the nation." A scan of the QR code gives the customers a chance to give live, real time feedback.

NARROW IT DOWN, BE SPECIFIC

Like at Jack Wills you need to draw up a picture of your perfect customer. Keep trying to narrow it down. Be more and more specific. This is the person you are going to be talking to in the brand pillar so the better you understand them the better your brand will be at communicating to them.

Don't worry about ruling out certain customers who often come in and spend good money. You're still going to give them a fantastic experience.

Jack Wills served many people outside their avatar. That's because the avatar was so narrow, so specific.

But, because we knew everything about Tom and Lucy, we could build a brand that spoke to them, and have product that appealed to them, and train our team to understand them so that when customers came shopping we had a range of product that they wanted to buy and an atmosphere they wanted to be a part of. It didn't matter that many of our customers were outside the avatar, what mattered was that we had identified a customer who was inside the avatar.

Customers both inside and outside your avatar will come precisely because of the brand you are building to serve your specific customer. A brand and an atmosphere in-store that they want to be a part of. Something they can aspire to. Something that makes them feel good and that they want to tell their friends about.

I love going to garden centres, I go no more than four times a year. But when I'm there I do a lot of daydreaming about what I could buy and I think about what our garden could look like if we had more time, space, and fewer kids' toys lying around.

I am not in their avatar. But I do spend money in garden centres. Their avatar is 60–70 years old, female, retired, income from a pension, her mortgage is paid off, she is fairly fit and healthy, her last holiday was a cruise to escape the UK winter. She has children who are working and grandchildren who are too young for school. Her interests are: holidays, wine, and of course being out in the garden. Last weekend she went to the theatre to see a new play and had a quick bite beforehand in a favourite restaurant.

Can you imagine this lady? Can you imagine her in the garden centre? It's important to narrow down exactly who your customer is and to know everything about them. It will not stop others from coming to your store.

You will constantly need to revisit this. Your brand will demand that you are checking back to ensure you know who your customer is, what they are thinking, doing, enjoying. Your customer's likes and interests will change with time and you need to know what that change looks like.

EXERCISE

Identify your customer:
How old are they?
Male or female? Or both?
How much money do they have?

Do they have children?
Are they homeowners or are they renting?
Are they employed, studying, retired?
Where do they go on holiday?
What did they do last weekend?
Where else do they spend their money?

2. LOYALTY

Now you have identified your customer you must ensure they know your business is a place they want to come to. You need to make sure they keep coming back. You need them to be loyal.

Loyalty works both ways. Think about the local essential food stores that stayed open during the coronavirus lockdown. There was a huge uplift in customers waiting patiently outside their local butchers and bakers and convenience stores. Once the pandemic started to subside, customers remained loyal to those stores. They hadn't been let down by them when they needed them most.

If you have a loyal customer, you need to ensure they are not enticed elsewhere.

Loyal customers spend more. Boots the chemist is one example of a brand with a loyalty card. They know that the ATV for loyalty card holders is significantly higher than the ATV for those who are not card holders. Boots regularly reward their card holders who in turn spend more money. Despite the discounts these customers are being given, they still spend more. Both customer and retailer are winning from their enhanced relationship.

THE VALUE OF A CUSTOMER

Let's think about the value of a single customer.

Start by understanding the lifetime value of a customer. If someone spends £40 a visit and they come in six times a year for 10 years, that's a £2,400 spend. Wouldn't you love this customer?

If someone comes into your coffee shop five days a week and spends £3.50 each time, are you going to love this customer? Would you learn their name and their favourite drink? Would you have it ready for them if they were always in a rush?

Of course you would. So, what are you going to do to make sure it's easy for them to come and shop with you?

LOYALTY PROGRAMMES

I've always admired Caffè Nero's simple loyalty programme. Every time you buy a hot drink, the barista puts a stamp on a small card. Once you have nine stamps your 10th drink is free. The card is business card sized so fits comfortably in a wallet or purse; consequently it's always with the customer and right next to the card or cash they are going to pay with anyway.

I also like that it pays back quickly; if you go in every day then once every two weeks their most loyal customers receive a free drink. I like that if I buy someone else a drink, I receive two stamps. The value is there every time I visit. What's more, it becomes a conversation piece, with eight stamps the barista points out: "You're nearly there." With nine stamps on: "Oh great, your next one's free." We've something to talk about other than my drinks order. We are building a relationship beyond the coffee transaction. A relationship built on loyalty from both sides.

It's app-based now although the physical business card is still available for those who haven't signed up to the app. The app brings a new layer of customer engagement and interaction. They can send messages to your phone. You can choose what messages you want to receive. More relationship building equals more loyalty.

Apps cost money and are great if you can justify the investment. But printing business cards costs very little and this could be rolled out in your business very easily.

You are continuously building a bigger picture of what is selling and who to.

An app is a powerful tool to have because you are capturing data. You know who your customer is and what they like to buy. If you can't produce an app, you must look at ways of capturing data about your customers. It will help you better understand who your customer is. Remember, you will constantly be checking back to see who your customer is and what's influencing their lifestyle; the data you capture will help shape your thinking.

Don't be afraid to try one technique for building loyalty and ditch it for another. Find the technique that works for your customer, and that they are engaged with. It could be a cashback incentive over a spend threshold that you offer to your best customers. It could be a discount. It could be something free like at Caffè Nero. Make sure it's convenient and drives repeat business.

DATA PROTECTION

Don't tie yourself in knots around GDPR. If your customer agrees to your collection and use of their data, it is held securely and can be deleted or provided to the customer if they request, then you should avoid any problems. If you're unsure then you should check with a lawyer or data protection expert.

EXERCISE

Create a loyalty programme:
What version of loyalty stamps card can you produce quickly for your business?
What will the incentive be for staying loyal to your business?
How will you capture your customers' data?
What have you learned from your customers' data?
What does this tell you about your customer?

3. REWARD YOUR CUSTOMER

Retailers have been rewarding their customers for years. It's so simple and highly effective.

My outdoor events teams would hand out glasses of champagne to our customers. The effect was incredible.

The alcohol goes to the head quickly and it loosens the mind. It was easier to persuade customers to try the clothes on, they were much more inclined to 'go for it', and because we'd given them a free gift, we'd invested in them, so there was a sense of exchanging value by purchasing something themselves. Win-win.

PEOPLE ATTRACT PEOPLE

Having a glass in hand made our customers stay longer. The champagne was simply a tool for holding people in the shop. We would turn the champagne on and off. When it was quiet, the champagne was brought out to draw in the crowd. We didn't mind if the first browsers didn't buy, we just kept them talking, literally about anything: the weather, the event, politics, we didn't care. Their job was to draw more people in, and then more. Eventually my staff would peel away from conversations and start helping customers to shop.

You can do this. And I'll let you into some secrets: it wasn't champagne it was cava, it didn't come in a proper glass but a plastic one, and we didn't give big glasses out. The power was saying to someone you've never met, "Can I offer you a glass of bubbles?" Very rarely does someone turn it down.

EXPERIENTIAL REWARDS

Retailers are taking the reward stage further and the clever ones are blending it into an experience that complements their product offer. Experiences give back to the customer something other than a gift. The effect is that customers spend more time in the store, building up more exposure to the brand and product, which in turn delivers enjoyment and trust with that brand.

I used to work with a store selling reclaimed furniture who ran furniture painting classes in the evenings after the store closed. At Sweaty Betty, the athleisure clothing retailer, they clear the shop floor after trade and host yoga and Pilates sessions. I know of sports footwear stores that have running groups. Beginners on one day, fun runners another day and the pro runners another day. There's a different experience for everyone.

At one of my clothing brands we would host product preview evenings at the start of a new season. We would invite local customers, media, and then our friends on consecutive Thursday nights at the start of the season. They would enjoy music, wine, and a convivial atmosphere as well as a 10% discount on purchases made that night.

Jack Wills majored in live music, promoting up and coming local bands who were given a platform on which to perform in the stores. We would host evening events, chuck in some drinks and snacks, and choose a venue for the afterparty. We were more interested in promoting the brand and providing a fun experience then selling clothes on the night. In fact, in one store we built a gig space in the basement, designed so that on gig nights we could hide the product away. We wanted the party to be epic, not to worry if someone was spilling vodka on the knitwear.

REWARDS BRING BENEFITS

Of course, the reason for rewarding your customer is to build that loyalty and ensure they keep coming back. You need to think of ways to ensure that you are always busy. There is always a way of making your stores busier still.

One of the mantras I have always remembered with customer service is this: "Customer service is what you receive, customer experience is what you feel." You can use customer experience to drive sales. The better the experience, the better the chance of repeat business and the greater the chance more people will be told about the experience.

How often do you phone your customers? If it's quiet this Wednesday morning what are you going to do to make sure it's not quiet next Wednesday morning? Very few companies do this, but for some companies it's an integral part of their business. When there are quiet moments in your store, rather than waiting for people to walk in or doing the cleaning, create a list of important customers who have shopped in the last few weeks and give them a call. If they don't answer, leave them a message. Very simply say "I'm just calling to see how everything is going with the [*insert product name*] that you bought from us the other day. We just wanted to make sure that you are enjoying it and if you have any questions about [*insert appropriate adjective* cleaning, maintaining, maximising, cooking, using, etc] it then we would be happy to help you."

Most people will say everything is fine, others may be grateful for the call and ask for advice. Very occasionally someone will gripe about it. In both these cases thank goodness you rang. You have just had a golden opportunity to improve their experience.

This isn't a sales call, it's a customer experience call. It's not about sales today, it's about future sales. You've taken the opportunity to remind them that you are there, and that you care about them and their investment. They won't forget.

Your customers are precious and should be protected and nurtured. Constantly do what is best for them. So many businesses go and chase new customers when the ones they already have are much more likely to buy again and again. Once you have them, wrap them in cotton wool. They are that precious.

Surprise them, delight them. Consider this: what can you give them that won't cost the earth but will make them feel special? I once hired a large river boat during Henley Royal Regatta and invited my best customers along for the day. We had drinks, canapes, a DJ, and some celebrities on board. It was great coverage for the brand in the magazine gossip columns of OK and Tatler. We had a photographer there who captured the day for us to re-live on social media afterwards. But much more important was the day out in the sunshine that we gave our customers. They had been loyal to us, so we rewarded them for being so.

EXERCISE

How can you reward your customer in a way that they will love?
What does your business do that you can teach your customer to do?
How are you going to build the time they spend with you?

Can you create an event where you surprise and delight your best customer?

SUMMARY

Make sure you revisit this chapter and please do the exercises. Understanding who your customer is will give you the edge over your competitors if you do it properly. Keep on refining them; make the description tighter and tighter. The success of your brand, which we cover in the next chapter, depends on you knowing as much as you can about your customer. Crucially, it will help your team to think about who they are talking to and how to talk to them, to level with them.

As time moves on and trends shift, you will need to constantly revisit your customer to ensure that you understand who they are today.

And don't worry about the customer who falls outside the description or demographic of your ideal customer. They will still come, precisely because they are attracted by what you do for your customer.

As you build loyalty with your customer you will ensure they keep coming back. The key to this is understanding each customer as best you can. The more bespoke you can make this to each individual, the better. Data and systems will help. But even in high volume places, like coffee shops and drink retailers, your people can learn what the customer likes and offer a personalised service.

Your customers are the very best advert for your brand. As I've said repeatedly, you need to nurture them and protect them; you cannot afford for a single one to go elsewhere if you are going to achieve your dreams. Find the reward that is right for your brand and your business. It doesn't need to be huge, but it does need to happen and the pay back is worth it.

Remember, customer service is what you receive, customer experience is what you feel. As the former Disney CEO said at that conference in the US: "Be a maniac about customer experience."

PILLAR 2: BRAND

To state the obvious, there is a direct correlation between having more people visit your stores and increasing your sales. There's nothing I hate more than the powerlessness and misery of a shop without customers. It's the reason we measure footfall first and then measure transactions; it measures our marketing. Every brand and marketing initiative in whatever form is designed to bring more customers to your store or website.

Think of your business as a brand. Whether you are a small convenience store that sells newspapers, or a farm shop or a women's fashion retailer. Your business is a brand.

Your aim is for your retail business to be overwhelmed with customers. You want customers queuing up for product launches or just to walk in on a normal day. Creating customer touchpoints across social media, local media, in-store, and out of store will drive the brand recognition all retailers need.

The purpose of this chapter is to encourage as many people to your stores as you can. Think about the lessons at the end of Part 1 in "The Science of Retail" chapter. This pillar on Brand is about driving customer traffic so you can increase the number of transactions you do in-store or online. This chapter also helps you build a business that people choose to shop from. Your penetration rate will improve because more customers have decided to do business with you before they've even walked into the store or logged onto the website.

The Brand pillar is built around three core parts: Brand Vision, Marketing, and Inspire. By the end of the chapter you will understand what your brand will need to look like to your customer, how you will market your brand to your customer, and how you will use your brand to inspire all those who touch your business: your people, your customers, and your suppliers.

WHAT MAKES A BRAND?

A great brand's strength is in its multiple touchpoints. Before I sample a brand, whether that's to visit, purchase or consume, I need to have heard about it, read about it or seen photos or video about it. In some way I need to have been inspired to interact with it.

Before you sample a brand and certainly before you invest in a brand you will need to be comfortable that it is safe to do so. This comes back to our most basic instincts around flight or fight. When we discover something unfamiliar, we are at first intuitively sceptical. If it seems safe or friendly, we might step closer and start to take more interest in it. If we are uncertain, we will turn away.

Think about the first time you pass a new neighbour. You might just nod at each other. The next few meetings will bring a shared greeting, a "Hello" or "Good morning". It could be after five or six interactions in which you have judged their character and deduced that they are not a nasty threat that you pause for a chat and start to properly know each other. After a couple more chats you might invite them over for a drink.

Over each stage you have built familiarity, likeability, and trust. The signals you have picked up have assured you that it's worth your while investing in this relationship.

Building this familiarity, likeability, and trust is precisely what you are doing when you build a brand.

GREAT BRANDS

Brands must be clear, focused, and specific about who they are and what they stand for. The customers of great brands will know precisely what they are buying when they shop with that brand. Zara's fashion is always on trend. Neptune's furniture is at the forefront of household design. Pret A Manger's food is fresh and quick. What does your brand epitomise? Your brand influences how people describe you and your business, and how they feel when they think about you and your business.

Whilst sad, it's not a total surprise that Jamie's Italian restaurants struggled. Because Jamie is from the UK I'm not going to go to him for an authentic Italian experience when there are so many Italian restaurants to choose from. Its failure was also a case of there being too many Jamie's Italians. If he had one in London and one in Manchester, I suspect they would still be here today, and customers would be booking tables weeks in advance.

Having a brand direction is crucial. Therefore, it is essential to start with your customer and to know precisely who they are and what motivates them. The brand is responsible for delivering on this again and again. If you are not crystal clear about your customer, you can't ever steer your brand in the right direction.

1. BRAND VISION

Your brand tells your customers or prospective customers who you are, what your credentials are, what you stand for, what's important to you.

Think about familiar brands and describe them and what their brand says to you. For me Apple is about innovative technology, slick design, and a world of opportunity. Virgin is about adventure, youthfulness, fun, and disrupting the norm. Selfridges is about newness, aspiration, exclusivity, ground-breaking design, and class.

Brands need to be authentic and transparent. Show what you do and how.

I spent some time meeting with 'wagamama' when I was looking at restaurant brands to bring into the airports. I was highly impressed with the thought and dedication that they have put into that business. It was no surprise when they told me they had grown like for like sales every month for the last six years. I made the following observations about their brand:

Their branding is visually strong, clear, and consistent across all their imagery, menus, and marketing collateral. The brand colours are used repeatedly, and they never move away from them. They have innovative content across multiple media channels that keeps the brand interesting and aspirational. The more videos I watch and the more photos I see and the more content I read the more I want to try new dishes and sample new flavours. Their messages talk to their purpose. They talk with care and consideration about things that matter to their brand, be it veganism, LGBT, or sustainability. They don't just chuck these words out there because they want to score points with certain customers. It's done with purpose because they truly care about these things. They tell stories about their brand that people can engage with, whether it's about the farms that their food comes from, the stories of the chefs that create the food, the history of the recipes in pan-Asian culture or even how you can cook the food yourself at home.

The 'wagamama' brand resonates with their customer. They know who their core customer is, and their message speaks to that customer continuously. Can you see how the thought and dedication to their brand vision shines through?

BRAND PRINCIPLES

What is your business known for? Think about brands you know and love and those that you maybe know and don't love so much. Ryanair divides most people. They are known for exceptional prices. Their planes leave on time and across Europe they travel to more places than any other airline. They are not known for customer service; however, this doesn't really bother them. They know they can compete on price. Always.

Your principles will be obvious to you, you need to make sure they are obvious to your customers. Here are just a few; consider where your brand stands on the following:

Price – low; mid; high

Ethical – we care; we care a bit; not that important to us

Sustainable – this is important; fairly important; we're not bothered about being sustainable

Charitable – we believe in giving back where we can; occasionally we give something back; we don't want to give back

Product – innovative; exclusive; widely available; run of the mill; famous brands; reliable; locally sourced

Customer service – we go above and beyond; we do the best job we can; we just transact, we don't serve

People – highly trained, passionate enthusiasts of our brand; well-selected people who care about doing a good job; a job's a job, I do my eight hours and leave

You need to choose what is important to you and your brand, and make sure that this will resonate with your core customer. This needs to be authentic; you can't make things up that are not true. It's not just that that's unethical, but you will be found out. Your customer will see through it if it's not true.

The brand must align with the customer. Once you have settled on what is important then keep coming back to it, explore it again and again. Talk with purpose about it, tell stories about it. Make sure it comes through in your marketing.

LASTING IMPRESSIONS LAST

When someone touches your business, what impression will they have of your brand?

Is it:

- **Fun, sensible, dry?**
- **Warm, cold, welcoming?**
- **Youthful, middle aged, grown up?**
- **Innovative, market leading, safe?**

You can shape this through your tone of voice, your style of artwork and imagery, your means and style of communicating.

THE FIVE SENSES

Think about the first interaction you had with that new neighbour. Your senses were on overload trying to pick up information that would tell you whether to run away or proceed with caution. We rely on our senses to guide us.

The five senses are sound, sight, taste, smell, and touch and the organs associated with each sense send information to the brain to help us understand and perceive the world around us. In a store environment and online we can deploy positive messages to please our customers' sensory receptors.

Sound – shops with music playing that appeals to their target customers will ensure they stay longer in-store. Consider what music your customer enjoys listening to and put a playlist together. What volume is this going to be: soft or loud? What is best for your demographic? If you've ever visited Abercrombie and Fitch's UK store on Saville Row it seems like you are walking into a night club; it's dark with targeted lighting, the music is very loud rock and teen classic tunes. Online, videos with appropriate music playing will shape your brand in the ears of your customers.

Sight – what do your displays look like? Do they make your customers want to come in and sample your product? Walk into any branch of Gail's Bakery and it's like a work of art. The displays are phenomenal and the multitude of cakes, breads, and pastries on display look heavenly. You can't help but want to try new things. Big brands have visual merchandising departments who are dedicated to ensuring the displays in-store look fabulous, and the windows tell the story of the season and hint at what is inside. How you display your product needs to match the essence of your brand. It is designed to draw as many people into store as possible. Compare the high piles of clothes in Sports Direct against the minimalistic approach of a fashion boutique. The message in the display shapes the perception of the shopping environment.

Taste – this is imperative for a food and drink retailer who can always have samples available for customers to taste, particularly at quiet times to draw a crowd, but also to allow customers to try new things. How better to entice customers in? But it also can be used for non-food and drink brands. My clothing brand gave away a glass of bubbles to our customers. Hairdressers often offer beer or wine to their customers. I know of retailers with mini self-serve coffee bars on the side to create the right shopping environment and encourage customers to stay longer.

Smell – is there anyone who doesn't love the smell of a bakery? You walk in and instantly are transported back to your childhood and wanting to buy a bun or a cake. It's very powerful.

Abercrombie and Fitch spray fragrances from their men's and women's range that they know appeals to the teenage target customer. Some shops have candles burning away. Others like the retailers mentioned above have the smell of coffee. What smells complement your brand? Think about how this can be incorporated into your store.

Touch – for most retailers this is the easiest to deploy. But make sure there are no barriers to touching. Clothes, where possible, should be easy to try on so customers can both touch and see what they look like. Walk into any homewares store and you want to feel the weight of the products. Your product is what you are trying to sell, so make sure the customer can touch and feel it.

The five senses help you to position your brand. Subconsciously your customer is always sizing up what they think about your brand and your product; you can heavily influence their perceptions of both.

Allow yourself time to pause and look around your stores; interact with them as though you're a customer visiting for the first time. This is hard if you are there every day, so take a step back and assess what your senses are telling you. Are all the senses being activated to best represent your brand?

BRAND GUIDELINES

Have rules for your brand imagery and stick to them. Ensure everyone in your team understands the rules and complies with them.

Choose what colours you will use; each shade has its own pantone reference. Don't go overboard on how many colours you use in your brand. Equally it doesn't need to be just one. Once you have chosen, stick with it.

Choose what font you will use and what font size is acceptable in each form of communication, and stick with it.

Limit how many logos you have. You want your customer to build up familiarity with your brand. It doesn't need to be just one, but again avoid having too many.

Once you have settled on colours, fonts, logos, and anything else that reflects the name and image of your brand then you must stick to it consistently. It should be the same on your email footers, letter heads, carrier bags, shop front signage, web page, brochures, dispatch forms. The same logo needs to appear on each social media channel. If you change one, you need to change them all. Don't ever make it hard for your customer, as they are building up trust and familiarity.

EXERCISE

What words describe familiar brands like Apple, Harrods, Greggs, Starbucks?
What are your brand principles?
Do you think your principles are obvious to your core customer?
What words describe your brand?
What lasting impressions will your customer have of your brand?
Is your branding consistent across every customer touch point?

What rules will you insist on for your branding? Think about logos, colours and fonts.
How can you deploy the five senses to make your brand appeal to your customer?

2. MARKETING

Many clients we speak to worry about marketing. Mostly this is based on a lack of experience which is perfectly understandable. There are so many hats you need to have to be a successful retailer, it's no surprise that this is not an area of strength. It doesn't need to be difficult, but it does have to be done.

As we discussed in the chapter: "Harness the Power of the Digital Revolution", if you don't have the time or the expertise then you should outsource it. But if you're interested or don't want to make the investment, then there are loads of books, some brilliant podcasts, of which I highly recommend *I Love Marketing* by Dean Jackson and Joe Polish, and plenty of videos on YouTube that you can binge on.

KEEP CREATING AND PUBLISHING CONTENT

The trick is to put content out and measure how well it's landed with you customers. Across multiple touch points you are looking to grow that familiarity, likeability, and trust. The more content you put out the better. When we discussed social media, we looked at having regular content created and posted by your social media team, be that you, or someone you have outsourced it to.

You can choose one thing to promote this week and repurpose it across video, photos, long stories, short stories, podcasts. You are trying to find the way that the message lands best with the customer.

You will settle on techniques that work well; although, you must not sit still because the customer won't and until they are queuing up at the door you still have work to do.

What you should avoid is trying to permanently sell. That is a huge turn off for customers. In order to balance this, you need to tell stories about your brand that will make people want to learn more. Tell stories about your employees or your suppliers. Tell stories about your customers. I remember posting a photo of some ducks that had brought traffic to a standstill outside a store of ours and by far it was the most liked and commented on post we put out that week. The great advantage of social media is that you can have a conversation with your customers.

When I say don't sell, I don't mean don't promote your product. If you're a butcher and have some steaks marinated ready for barbecuing ahead of a long, hot weekend, then that's great and you should promote it. What no one wants to see is wall to wall pictures of products with a 'buy now' message on.

When I ran an event on a boat during Royal Henley Regatta, we took photos and made videos which were released over many days after the event. The engagement in our brand both before and afterwards was superb.

If you are nervous about marketing, then follow brands on social media and in the press that will matter to your customers. Look at how others are using headlines or a call to action and try this in your business. Brands are being incredibly active and interactive on social media. Promoting products, showcasing content so people know what's available. Instagram and Facebook are integral to this. I have very little interest in cosmetics on a personal level, but I follow MAC on Instagram. I'm continuously impressed by the quality of the content they produce. A cursory glance each day will fill you with ideas for your business.

BUILDING FAMILIARITY, LIKEABILITY, AND TRUST

Whatever you do, don't do nothing. Put out content. The more content the better. It will all help to build the story of your brand. The more content customers can find about you, whether it's video, images, stories, or podcasts, the more they will be inclined to buy.

Slowly but continuously you will be building familiarity, likeability, and trust. The more content there is, the more your customers can read and watch and learn about who you are and what sort of business you are to purchase from.

The content you put out remains in the public domain unless you remove it. It's continually, layer by layer building your brand asset. By constantly building familiarity, likeability, and trust you are creating a mini ecosystem that will pay you back many years after the content that went into it was created.

FIND THE RIGHT PLATFORM

Marketing has been described to me as being like drilling for oil. You need to keep looking in different places for the oil. Once you find oil, keep going back down the well again and again. It's the same with marketing. You need to find the platform that works for your customers.

Once you've found that platform, then use it again and again. It could be social media, it could be email campaigns, it could be a regular advert in the local parish magazine, it could be a flyer through customers' doors. Keep trying them all.

TEST AND MEASURE

The goal of marketing is to find the message that brings in the customers. What you think is the right message may not be for your customer and the only way you will know is to split test. You need to be creating and deploying five or six messages with the same promotion but keep varying the headline, image, text or call to action. Online you can use different redemption codes to see which advert the customer is responding to. In-store you can use redemption codes but also you can ask where they saw the advert. You might find one product responds better to the same headline and promotion than another. The only way to know this is to test various options and measure the results. It's the only way you will know how your marketing is working.

TONE OF VOICE

'innocent' smoothies have a very chatty, tongue-in-cheek approach to their tone of voice. If you read the back of their bottles there are little jokes dotted about. It adds value and for them it ticks the likeability box with their customer. Many brands have tried to emulate this and to be honest it doesn't look authentic; it looks like they are copying 'innocent'. Once you have a style to your tone of voice, you should stick with it. It will help create and build the familiarity and trust.

STYLE OF ARTWORK AND IMAGERY

As with your tone of voice, you should find a style to your artwork and photography that is consistent and resonates with the brand. If you are going to use moody lighting or black and white images, then you should be consistent. The tools on our phones allow us to be creative and you should have fun doing so, but make sure it reflects your brand and once you have settled on it you stick to it.

MARKETING BECOMES ADDICTIVE

Don't let marketing overwhelm you. Its job is to bring customers to your stores. You mustn't avoid it on the grounds of cost either. It is an investment that pays off.

You can limit the spends on your digital marketing. If you are measuring the results you will know how well it's working.

Be patient, it will take time. In part this is because you are learning and trying new techniques, but also because the algorithms that run search engines and social media channels take a while to pick up the content you are putting out and matching it with the customers who are looking for it.

As you do more and more testing and measuring, you will likely become addicted to it. I know of many retailers who wake up in the night to see how many likes or comments a post has had, or to see how a product is selling off the back of an advert they have placed.

Your goal is to create a community who are regularly interacting with your brand. They are slowly but surely building that familiarity, likeability, and trust.

When the time is right, they will be ready to buy.

EXERCISE

Ask your customers what social media they use.
Create a profile across your selected social media platforms which is branded consistently.
Choose a theme or topic for the week and create content around it.
Measure the results of your marketing.

3.   INSPIRE – CUSTOMERS, PEOPLE, SUPPLIERS

A brand has meaning to everyone who touches it. It provides purpose and direction to its people and suppliers. It should provide trust and reassurance in its product to its customers and it should inspire everyone. There are some notable exceptions who don't seek to inspire. Ryanair springs to mind again, but the opportunities their affordable flying provides can be inspirational to their customers.

In truly great businesses the brand is their most valuable asset. Assets have value and if you wanted to sell your company then this asset will contribute to the fee you can command.

One of your aims as an independent retailer is to establish yourself as the expert in your space. Leverage the trust customers have in local stores. No one can know your product like you do, why you selected it, what its provenance is, why it is special. Draw this out in your communications; it will reinforce your expertise, positioning you as highly knowledgeable in this sector. The big high street brands with multiple stores cannot compete with an independent when it comes to expertise because they cannot possibly train all their staff to be on message across such a wide product range. Make sure your customer knows that you are the expert and can be trusted. The marketing content you put out as an independent retailer must continuously reinforce the concept of you and your business as experts in your space. It will draw customers to you, and it will allow you to command higher prices.

BRAND AND CUSTOMERS

All the thinking in the first two sections of the Brand pillar is done to inspire your customers. To build familiarity, likeability, and trust and to create the ecosystem of content that will layer on layer build the aesthetic of your brand, drawing out the principles you will be and are known for. Principles that reflect the wants and needs of your target customer.

BRAND PIECE LIFE CYCLE

Your product will bring your brand to life. In your range you should have certain product lines that do a job for your brand at any given moment. It could be warming soups in winter in a coffee shop, or brightly coloured shrubs in spring in a garden centre. Product lines that epitomise your brand to your specific customer.

I developed the Brand Piece Life Cycle concept below to show how this comes alive within a retail business.

BRAND PIECE LIFE CYCLE

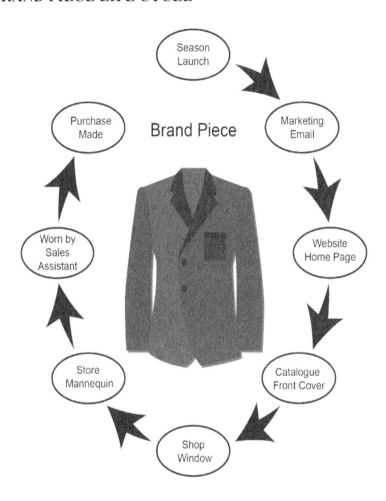

Let's look at this through the eyes of a customer of one of my clothing brands. It's the start of a new season and we have chosen a navy boating blazer with our logo on the breast pocket and white piping down the lapels and on the collar and cuff. It has a bright red, white, and blue inner lining and has been designed by a legend of Jermyn Street. It is the brand piece that will epitomise that season.

One morning lying in bed the customer opens an email from us. In the email is an image of a guy wearing that blazer. It looks awesome. The customer clicks the link that takes him to the homepage of our website; there is the blazer again being worn by the model. The customer really likes this blazer. He's going to Royal Henley Regatta this year and that's exactly what he wants to wear. That morning he goes downstairs and picks up the post, there is a catalogue from us and on the front page is that model again wearing that awesome blazer. The customer heads out to meet a friend and walks past our store; in the window he sees that blazer again. The customer walks into the store passing a mannequin with the blazer on and is greeted with a cheery "Good morning" by a member of the store team who is busy folding clothes, looks like the model in the pictures, and is also wearing the blazer. The customer starts to browse and 15 minutes later walks out of the store having made a purchase.

What did he buy? The blazer? No. Highly unlikely. That blazer cost £349 and we are not going to sell that many. The customer walked out with a £39 t-shirt.

The blazer did a job. It re-enforced the principles of the brand in the eyes of the customer. It reminded them of themselves and what they like and how they want others to perceive them. It spoke to them on a level they understood. The blazer inspired the customer to come into the store, it drove footfall, and it drove a transaction. It doesn't matter that he didn't buy the blazer; what matters is that the blazer epitomised the brand and brought customers into the store.

Brand pieces don't need to be best sellers, but they need to tell stories and connect emotionally with your customer.

BRAND AND PEOPLE

Your customer is not the only stakeholder you need to inspire. Without great people and great suppliers your business will not move out of first gear. A strong brand will attract great people which will allow you to build great teams. Companies will want to work with you and partner with you as they see how your brand principles and brand appeal allies with their customer. I now want to investigate further how your brand can help your business grow by harnessing your people and your suppliers.

Your brand is an asset and it is this asset that is the glue that holds a great business together. It ensures everyone is pulling together in the same direction. Can you imagine how powerful that is to have all your people on the same page pulling in the same direction?

Sorting your brand is an efficient way of sorting your people. If you have an inspirational brand that is very popular with its target customer, then you will have no problems attracting new staff who are already eulogists for your brand.

BRAND AND CULTURE

Your brand and your culture need to match because if they don't the customers will see through it. Your people are the public face of your business; if they are inspired to work hard for the brand then the brand will benefit. It becomes a self-fulfilling circle. Good brands attract good people who do a good job and the brand does better attracting more customers who spend more money, demand goes up and you need more good people.

Creating the right culture that fits with your brand will pay you back. Your people will want to work for you and the brand will establish itself far quicker. Spend time establishing a culture that rewards people for being brilliant, and a place that people want to jump out of bed and go and work for.

UTILISE AMBASSADORS

In a cluttered world with so much noise and information around us through multiple forms of media it can be hard to cut through and reach your customer.

A technique I've used successfully is to identify people who epitomise my brand perfectly. They look right, and they are into the same things as my customers. You know who your customer is, what they like and are inspired by, what trends influence them, so match this up with a well-known personality who can become an ambassador for your brand.

In both my clothing businesses I brought in incredibly talented sports stars, including Olympic gold medallists to represent the brand. They would talk about our brand, wear our clothes, turn up at customer events, and we would leverage their name. All for virtually no cost.

Because they were already widely known, liked and respected, they could quickly tap into new audiences that would have taken far longer for our brand to cut through to.

116

Many brands are using influencers. An influencer is someone who has built up a large following on social media. They attend all the relevant events in their industry and when they speak about it, others pay attention. The instant sales seen from events attended by the right influencers can be immensely powerful for a brand.

Finding the right local or national ambassador for your brand will speed up the growth of your brand. They can bring the familiarity; you then build the likeability and trust.

BRAND AND SUPPLIER

In the next chapter we will investigate the relationship you have with your suppliers. Suppliers are a key part of the ecosystem you are creating within your business. If you can explain to them what your brand principles are, who your customer is, and how you communicate with them the better your suppliers will be able to serve you. Key suppliers want to be a part of your success. If they know what is important to you and your customer, then they will be able to make and produce a range of product that fits your demographic.

You should think carefully about how you bring your suppliers in on your brand's direction, your philosophy; if this is well harnessed then they can help make your valuable brand asset more successful for you.

Some brands will host annual or bi-annual events where they talk to all their suppliers together. Maybe there is a serious part to the morning and then something entertaining to do in the afternoon where everyone can relax. I know of one retailer who takes all his suppliers to the races every year. They start in a hotel for a two hour seminar where he tells them how his business is performing, where the business is heading, and ensures they understand his customer and his brand. Once the important business update is complete, they head off for an afternoon of fun. He knows his best suppliers look forward to the day. It keeps them loyal to him and he also knows that the better they understand his business and what he is trying to achieve, the better they can support him to achieve his goals.

I asked him if it ever concerned him that all the suppliers know one another, and he replied that "On balance I figured they all know what each other's strengths are; for me I could see the value in having good loyal suppliers who understood our business. There would be times when I needed them to help me, be that on a new product idea or extended payment terms."

Involve your suppliers in your brand. They are a valuable part of your business; they will understand you better and they will also be ambassadors for what you do. The better you do, the better they do. They know this and they want to see you succeed.

EXERCISE

How will you explain your brand to your people?
Ask your people how they will explain your brand to your customer?
Create an onboarding document for all your people to read and sign up to. A set of principles that they will live by to always be the best ambassadors of your brand. What will your brand culture mean to your people?

Who has a following that fits your customer profile that can be an ambassador for your business? Draw up a shortlist and approach them.
What items in your product range will be a brand piece for you?
How will you deploy this brand piece in your marketing?
How will you explain your brand to your suppliers?
Ask your suppliers what it's like to work with your brand.

SUMMARY

Your brand is an asset. Like you would with your home, you need to keep investing in it, maintaining it, and improving it. Assets make money and a brand is no different. The stronger your brand asset is, the greater your business becomes.

Brands create the demand. To have customers you need them to want to come in. The first thing I said in this chapter was there is a direct correlation between having more people visit your stores and increasing your sales. Your job every day is to keep reinforcing that need for your customers, both new and existing, to come to your online and offline stores. The more time you invest in building the familiarity, likeability, and trust in your brand, the more sales you will make.

Guided by the needs and wants and inspirations of your customer, go and establish your brand vision. What are the principles that underpin this? Be consistent and keep going as you will increase the awareness in your brand. Don't be afraid of marketing; try new things and test and measure the results. Finally share the brand vision by inspiring your most important stakeholders: your customers, your people, and your suppliers.

You will always be revisiting your brand. It's such a powerful asset and needs nurturing and caring for. But it will continuously pay back as you become a successful retailer.

PILLAR 3: PRODUCT

You know your product far better than I do. I can't tell you what product to sell. For most retailers the product they sell goes right back to their core, their reason for starting and running this business in the first place, be it making cake or a love of fashion.

Unfortunately, and you already know this, your passion for your product won't be matched by all your customers. Damn them! But that's ok. Your job, with your carefully selected product mix, is to make them want your product as much as you want them to buy it; putting money in your till. Your job is to create want.

At Jack Wills we sold an enormous amount of underwear. The girls' knickers were not called knickers. 21-year-olds don't buy knickers, their grandmothers do, and they go to Marks and Spencer for those. 21-year-olds buy what the Jack Wills's marketing team called boy pants. The photo of the model in the boy pants made it quite certain that this was the only kind of underwear you should be wearing. The Jack Wills marketing team made the female customers want those boy pants. No one needed them, but every customer wanted them. Your job with your product mix allied with your marketing strategy is to create want.

Product completely brings your brand to life. Product is the essence of your business that customers can consume, touch, and feel. Your brand has slowly built familiarity, and it has worked hard to bring that customer into your store either online or offline.

Once they have made a purchase you can build the trust. Trust in your brand, trust in your product.

The Product pillar is built around three core parts: Range, Source, and Margin. By the end of the chapter you will understand the role of your product in making your business successful, and you will see the value that lies within your product range and how to extract that value to put cash into your bank account.

1. RANGE

THE PRODUCT LIFE CYCLE

You know who your specific customer is, what they like, what they are interested in. Your brand continuously speaks to this customer; it reflects them and their interests. Now it is up to your carefully selected product to fulfil their wants and needs.

There needs to be a strategy to your product range. The strategy needs to be considered in light of who your customers are and what your brand represents. Before you start buying your product you need to have a direction of travel; the buying needs to reinforce both the customers' needs and your brand. To bring the three pillars of Customer, Brand, and Product together you need to consider the life cycle of your product.

THE PRODUCT LIFE CYCLE

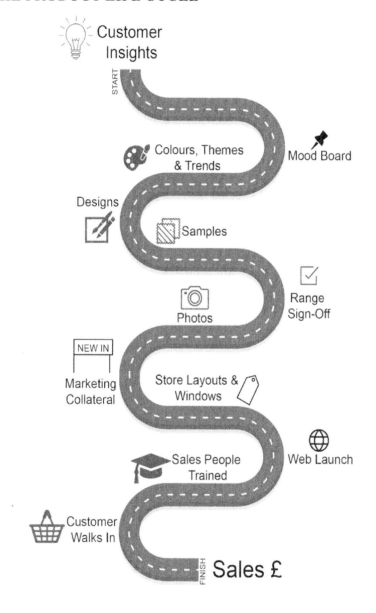

Let's say a new year has just started and you and your team are planning what you will sell this autumn. The Product Life Cycle starts with your customers' insights; you know what they like and what autumn means to them. In a café this could be warm soups made from freshly harvested vegetables, in a fashion brand it's knitwear and coats, in a butcher it's beef stew and slow cooking. A mood board is pulled together with images of what autumn means to your customers. Colours, themes, and emotions are layered onto the mood board. Product is designed that matches the emotions and themes from the mood board; product that matches the customer, the brand, and the season. Soon samples come back from suppliers who have been well-briefed about the essence of the forthcoming season. You test and taste and try on; ideally you show this to a select group of customers and garner their feedback on your strategy and direction of travel. With feedback and sampling complete, you sign off the product range for this autumn, you agree what the best sellers will be and how much quantity to buy, and you agree what the brand pieces will be that tell the story of that season. Photos are taken and the marketing collateral is created. This is the content that you will be pushing out to your customers throughout the autumn season.

As the season nears, it's time to plan the store and website look and feel. The shop window and home page need to truly encapsulate the feeling of that season; the emotions, and themes you agreed back in January need to be brought to life for your customers. Inside the store the layout needs to reinforce the messages you've given through your marketing and window and web displays. Can you smell the soups? Can you imagine the beef stews bubbling away? Are the coats on the mannequins wrapped up for a bracing walk through the wind and leaves?

Now it's time to train your people. They need to fully buy into the message of this season. Inspire them to feel the emotions of autumn; the tastes and trends and themes will be brought to life through their future engagements with the customers. Make sure they are as inspired now as you were back in January. Now it's time to open the doors, launch the new product on the website, and let the customers in. The selling starts. Listen to what they say, measure the sales, tweak the price if you must. Gather as much feedback as you can. Just think, in two months' time it will be January and you'll be starting all over again.

Your product sells your brand. Use your product to tell stories. The blazer example I gave in the Brand Piece Life Cycle in the previous chapter was made in East London, a stone's throw from the Olympic Park, designed by a Jermyn Street designer and incorporated a brilliant red, white, and blue lining that screamed British heritage. This blazer was something we talked about continuously; our staff wore it, it sat in windows, we sent it out for PR. It was designed as a brand piece. It doesn't matter how many brand pieces you sell, what matters is the effect they have on your other products. Once the brand piece has brought customers into your store and website you can start selling all the other products you have.

This planning process and the strategy for the next quarter, season or selling window are crucial and should not be overlooked. I can tell quickly when I enter a store whether the retailer truly strategically cares about what they are selling or whether the approach is haphazard.

As a smaller independent retailer, you need to be known for what you do and be regarded as an expert. Your product range can give you this authority and credibility. Fully understanding your purpose and the direction of your strategy allows your people to explain to your customers the essence of the season you are in, the thinking that's gone into the range, and what it means for them. By doing this you will create trust in your product and your brand in the eyes of your customers.

YOUR ONLINE RANGE

You can use your web stores to test new products in front of your customers before actually investing in them. Increasingly suppliers and retailers are working collaboratively to pitch new products that they don't want to commit to buying upfront.

You can have more product online than in your shops. For example, you can buy one colour of a style for your store and sell the other colours online. If your suppliers can work with this strategy, it's a huge benefit to you. This can also be used as an 'online exclusive' marketing message. Your catalogue grows, but your financial exposure is reduced. Some suppliers will not do this, but the forward-thinking ones may allow it on certain lines and particularly where they have over ordered themselves. It's a strategy that John Lewis uses to great effect and will benefit retailers of all sizes.

CONSUMERISM IN THE AGE OF EXPERIENTIAL

Talk to an influencer right now and they will tell you that customers want experiences rather than things.

126

Consumers are choosing possessions less and less. Increasingly they want experiences, such as adventurous holidays and fine dining experiences; they want to make memories. If your product is not an experience or memory maker then you need to make sure the purchasing of your product is just that. Customers need to be left with a feeling of wow. This is the added extra that goes above and beyond the product. A 'wow' that will ensure they tell their friends and that they come back for more. Look at the recent growth of bars where you can play indoor golf, darts, or ping pong. Look at the market halls opening with long bars on the side and multiple street food vendors in the middle. These food vendors change every few months to keep it fresh and innovative.

Richard Lim, CEO of Retail Economics, talks of "creating meaningful experiences". If I can go to a shop and be given dedicated time and space to make a considered purchase, then I'm likely to spend more money. Imagine buying an expensive watch or a suit; it's not a rushed decision. You can create an environment in the store where dwelling for as long as the customers want is encouraged.

Equally, if your product range constitutes basics or essentials, such as in a convenience store, then the experience of buying it needs to be memorable. How can you tweak the displays to be theatrical and impressive? Think about the five senses; what is your music system playing and at what volume, what smells greet me as I walk in?

In the age of Instagram, you as a retailer can introduce moments which encourage your customers to shout about your product and their experience in your store. This could be a carriage fit for a princess in the Disney store or a fantastic wicker chair hanging from the ceiling in a back-street café; any place that commands a photo and a #hashtag to your store.

I was talking at a conference in Helsinki where one of the other speakers, a young American, was eulogising about Instagram. She told the audience, "If you didn't Instagram it, it didn't happen." It's a useful insight into the mindset of the generation that wants to share what they are doing, where they are, and who they are with. It's all part of the experience. Their experience.

Experiences help you sell. That's why Sweaty Betty clear their shops and run yoga and Pilates classes. That's why the reclaimed furniture store ran painting classes. That's why the independent butcher organises offsite barbecue classes throughout the summer.

Don't be misled into thinking the rise of experiential is at the cost of consumerism. We live in a society that consumes. Experiential is a means of selling more product.

EXERCISE

Create your own Product Life Cycle. It doesn't need to be seasons. It could be a product launch or sale period.
Ask your suppliers what you can sell online that you don't have to purchase first.
What would your customers take a photo of in your store?
What experiences would a customer enjoy in your store and tell their friends about?

2. SOURCE

SOURCING PRODUCT

Most retailers source their product from suppliers. They will meet the supplier at a trade show or at their showroom. Often suppliers will have agents on the road who will come to the stores and head offices of the retailers. The meeting involves a showcasing of the product available, either in the form of samples or from a catalogue. Cost prices and RRPs (recommended retail price) are set out and typically there will be a uniform mark-up across the board. This varies from industry to industry, but you can expect the price the supplier sells at to be roughly 50% of the RRP. These suppliers are wholesalers. Often that's all they do. It's a trade price for one business to sell to another business who in turn sells to the customers.

When I ran clothing brands, we had a wholesale division that sat alongside our retail divisions. We had a showroom, agents on the road, and attended trade shows. It was incredibly useful for us to hear the market feedback on our forthcoming collections six months before it went into our own stores.

Based on the pre-sales we'd achieved through wholesale, we already knew what the best sellers would be when the range launched in-store. This meant we could increase the amount of product we bought on those lines.

BUY YOUR OWN

For those that can, please don't just source from other brands at wholesale rates. Go and make your own. It's never been easier to source your own product range. Create your own product, stick your own brand label on it, and start enjoying greater margins. Start simple.

The reason for this is margin. With our own product we would make a four to five times mark-up from the fully delivered cost price to the retail price. This meant when we wholesaled the product, we could double the price and then double it again for retail.

Cost price = £10
Wholesale price = £20
Retail price = £40/£50

The challenge in making your own product is order quantities. If the order is too small, factories will not touch it. But, don't be put off. Start with a product that has longevity and you can afford to sell over an extended period and source that.

You can source and design products from a multitude of suppliers without ever having to go on a plane. There are many trade shows across the UK that are attended by some of the more forward-thinking manufacturers. It's well worth trawling around these and looking for inspiration. For relatively little upfront cost you can be sampling your next range.

Food and drink venues can use their own recipes and ingredients to make their brand their own. Perhaps your brand piece is your iconic hot chocolate made from a specially sourced cocoa and finished with marshmallows. Or it's the cheese shop with their own chutneys sitting alongside their cheese range.

Where you can make your own product, you must. The margins are worth the effort and it's far easier to create the credibility in your brand that will build trust for your customers.

NEGOTIATE

Margin is the lifeblood of a retailer. Negotiate on every price. Then negotiate total order quantity discounts. Then negotiate early payment discounts. Then ask what extras your suppliers can give you for free. Negotiate on everything you buy. You cannot afford not to.

If the sales agent turns up with a price list, look at it with disdain, say that it's a useful indicator and put it to one side.

There are some excellent training courses in negotiation and these are well worth investing time in. I've made colossal sums and saved colossal sums for myself and others through skills acquired on negotiation courses and putting those skills into practice. It becomes very addictive.

There are books on the subject and I strongly recommend investing time in reading them through. I won't share all the techniques I've acquired here but a few effective tips are:

- Nothing is agreed until everything is agreed. Keep negotiating until you've squeezed them dry.
- Don't worry about them, only worry about yourself. They will know when they need to stop negotiating. Your job is to find that point.
- You can walk away from any negotiation. Always.
- Before you start negotiating, work out what you can give that they want. Work out what they can give that you want. These are known as levers. List all the levers that you have, and they have: time; cost; payment terms; delivery terms; discounts; promotion space; point of sale material; order quantity; etc, etc, etc.
- Silence. When you've asked for something shut up and let them speak. Don't say a word until they have spoken.
- Be comfortable with being uncomfortable. Negotiating is not a relaxed, comfortable place. Accept this and move on. Your business is on the line. Having to shut your business is far more uncomfortable.

There are so many levers that you can negotiate on.

i.   Asking for payment discounts is always a good place to start. If you have cash in your business, offer to pay within two to five days of delivery and suggest a 5% discount to the supplier. They may well be cash strapped particularly having paid out for all their stock.

ii. Alternatively, if you are planning on placing a big order, ask for a volume discount. Draw out in advance what thresholds you will need to cross to trigger discounts.

iii. Another technique is to sell your prime selling space. Supermarkets do this all the time. Brands will offer favourable terms to be on the aisle ends. Equally they will give discounts to be on the shelves at eye level. You can adopt this in your store. If a supplier wants to be promoted in your store, then they should pay for the privilege.

iv. Ask them to give you free products to sell as a 'gift with purchase'. It will make it easier to sell and add value to the product, this benefits you and the supplier. The beauty sector uses this technique regularly. A free eyeliner or sample hand cream given with a spend of over £50 for example. This drives ATV and it rewards the customers.

v. Lastly, you could have a weekly campaign of products you lead with. They appear in your marketing collateral, on the homepage of your website, all over your social media. Why not share the benefits of doing this with the supplier? Ask them to contribute towards the marketing costs and layer on a discount for the volume of product you will shift. Can you see how you can make your marketing strategy align with your product strategy?

When it comes to selling, make your people aware that they have no latitude whatsoever to negotiate on price. If a customer wants a discount, then there are multiple ways of them having one. They can sign up to your database and be the first to hear about special offers and invites to pre-sale evenings or to season launch events where you offer special prices to your most loyal customers. Rather than saying no to the request for a discount, turn it into a positive.

LOVE YOUR SUPPLIERS

Whilst I've told you to negotiate very hard with your suppliers, you must also treat them with respect. Negotiating price is good sport and it is necessary business. If you say you will pay early, then do so. Suppliers are important stakeholders in your business.

Your suppliers will be ambassadors for your brand. They will be pleased to supply you and you should treat them with respect.

Great suppliers become partners and with partners you can do powerful things. You want your suppliers to have the same familiarity, likeability, and trust in your brand as you want your customers to have.

Suppliers work very hard to win your business; they care that you do well. They will often woo you with goodie bags, entertainment, nights away. Accept these and enjoy them; but know it comes with a goal: a hope that they will win your business. Corporate entertainment, be it a dinner in a restaurant or tickets to a football match, is a very powerful way to do business. Suppliers will do it for you and if you can, do it for them; it will make your relationship stronger. With a strong relationship built on shared interests outside of your business then good things follow. When an opportunity comes their way, they are much more likely to introduce it to their favourite retail partners. Equally, when you have an idea you need help with, your most loyal suppliers are more likely to take a punt on it because they know and like you.

It pays to look after your suppliers as well as you look after your customers.

3. MARGIN

So, as we've established, I can't tell you what product to buy into your stores. What the Product pillar sets out to do is help you extract more cash from the product you are selling. This pillar drives margin: the gap between your top-line sales and your bottom-line costs. It is often expressed as a percentage.

After your customers, margin is the only thing that matters in retail. Without customers and margin, you don't have a business. Carefully watching your margin is critical.

Margin is the difference between profit and loss, the difference between success and failure, the difference between spending time working in the business and working on the business. Margin allows you to take next week off to strategize what you will do next to drive sales in your business. You need to watch margin like a hawk.

PRICES

When was the last time you put your prices up? It sounds simplistic, but this is the quickest way to increase margin. On the whole, retailers cut prices in a bid to attract custom. This becomes an uncomfortable race to the bottom. Don't do it. Your customers will learn very quickly what your strategy is. Instead, put your prices up. Do this at least once a year. Aim for 5–10% on every item you sell. When in doubt, round the price up. Do this on every product. The cost of goods is going up, so must the price they are sold for. Congratulations, your sales have just gone up by 10%.

VALUE FOR MONEY

Think about the range of restaurants you can visit. You could go to McDonalds and spend £3–£5 per head and come away very well fed. You could also visit a Michelin starred restaurant and spend £300 per head. You would also leave feeling very well fed.

Both restaurants have provided exactly what was expected of them at totally different prices. The difference is value for money.

If you have an incredible restaurant location with views overlooking the sea, expensive food but poor customer service and the food comes out slowly, is cold and is delivered at different times from everyone else on your table, then you will leave feeling dissatisfied. You will not tell people to go there; you may even tell people not to go there.

However, if the service is incredible, the food is exceptional, the staff are friendly, and the atmosphere leaves you wanting more, then you will absolutely go back there. You will tell other people to go there. You will even not mind being told there is a 30 minute wait when you arrive there; you know it will be worthwhile as you can see the restaurant is full of other diners having a great time. The food is the same expensive price, but that's not what everyone is talking about. They are talking about the wonderful atmosphere and great food and customer service. You receive excellent value for money.

ESTABLISH YOURSELF AS THE EXPERT

The price will diminish in importance when you focus on quality of product, great service, understanding the needs of your customers and creating an attractive brand where customers are inspired to spend their money. The more customers that come to your store and the longer customers must wait can also, in the right circumstance, add value to the product being bought. I know of butchers and bakers where people queue for 20 minutes to go inside; it doesn't diminish from their experience and they are not put off by the prices that are higher than the alternative nearby butchers and bakers. Once they are inside, they are treated brilliantly, the team working there are knowledgeable and polite, and the food is excellent. It is worth the wait.

As an independent retailer you are far better off establishing yourself as the expert in your space, be it floristry, bakery, coffee, fashion, etc. Your expertise, knowledgeable teams, and fantastic brand will attract customers and will command a higher price. Customers will value your insights and the experiences they have shopping with you. They will be happy to spend money with you because of the service and experience they have when they do so. Your expertise adds value to the product. High street brands with multiple stores cannot provide this expertise or command those prices. Their product range will be far wider, and their staff spread thinner as they inevitably try to cover more and more bases to justify their large shop and expensive rents.

THE ROLE OF THE MERCHANDISER

In big retailers there will be a buying and merchandising department. Whereas the store and website teams' performances are measured on sales, the buyers' and merchandisers' performance is measured on margin. The buyers' job is to buy product at the right price, and the merchandisers are the geniuses behind it all who choose what price the product will sell for. They will choose which store receives which products and in what quantities.

The merchandiser reviews sales daily and weekly. If a product is selling very quickly, they will be on to the buyers to bring in some more. If a product is not selling quickly enough, they will be on to the sales teams to push it harder. They are constantly deciding which product needs pushing harder, or which product to buy more of. Identifying best sellers and ensuring that the sales teams in all store and web locations know what the good products are, and that the customers are equally well-informed.

Every week you should dedicate time to review your inventory. Look at sell through rates, look at margins, and take decisions. The data is very powerful. Merchandisers talk about 'weeks' cover'.

If you bought 100 of this item and sold 10 in the first week then you have nine weeks' cover left. This insight helps you choose what stock sits where in the store. You are looking to extract as much value and cash from your inventory all the time. It is essential you pay attention to the data.

Now, tell your stores and web teams what the best sellers are, which lines to put in which places in the stores or at the top of a product page online. You need to give your sales teams insights based on data as frequently as possible. This needs to be at least once a week.

The merchandiser manages the end of season sale. They choose which products are going into the sale and what price they will sell at. The merchandiser then watches how well each product performs at its new price. If further markdowns in price are required to start selling more of a certain line then the merchandiser will action it. They are always watching their individual product margins and their overall margin for the whole range.

They know at the end of the season their bonus will depend on them delivering as much money from each line of product as they can. They also need to do this with as little product left at the end of the season as possible.

That's why they are geniuses and that's why big retailers pay good money for good merchandisers. They deliver on margin.

GOOD, BETTER, AND BEST PRICES

You know from your data which lines are giving you the best sales and bringing in the most cash. You also know which lines are giving you the best margins. Now make sure your staff know this. If you have a line that has a great margin, then you need to be selling as much of it as possible. Tell your staff where to focus their attention, and which lines you want them to push.

Once you have an item or line that's selling well, look to see if you can increase the margin on it. This is where you have essentially the same line at multiple prices. Examples would be the branded Heinz baked beans positioned alongside the supermarket baked beans. The branded baked beans command a higher price.

Sandwiches are another great example. At an airport you can buy a packaged cheese and ham sandwich from Boots or WHSmith for £2.99. Or you can go to a coffee shop and pay £3.99 for a cheese and ham sandwich. That same coffee shop could also sell a premium cheese and ham baguette with a few salad leaves and English mustard at £5.99.

At London Stansted Airport, one of the food and beverage retailers typically sold 350 cheese and ham sandwiches a week. They decided to introduce a premium option that cost £2 more. They still sold 350 a week but 20% of them were now sold at the higher price with a greater margin. In pure sales terms they now took £140 extra a week, equating to £7,280 extra a year from the sale of cheese and ham sandwiches.

Without increasing penetration, sales increased by driving ATV.

By providing greater value you can command higher prices. Start with good products at an entry level price, better products at a mid-level price and your best products at a premium level price. This will add value to your product range and drive increased margin from what is essentially the same product.

There will always be customers who want a premium service or experience and you need to leverage that desire. You can position certain lines as exclusive – maybe it can only be found in your stores – or you could position a line as being a limited edition. Once they are gone, they are gone. In both instances you could charge a premium price, produce marketing content around these products, and drive a great customer experience around them to match. Just by taking an ordinary product you can reposition it to do a special job for you.

EXERCISE

Analyse and interrogate your stock inventory. What is your average margin percentage? What are the highs and lows in your margin?

Put your prices up. What is your new margin?

Refer to the Brand pillar: is your expertise obvious from your marketing?

Look at your inventory and stock management system every week. Dedicate time to review the data and make decisions based on your results.

What products that you sell could warrant a good, better, and best price?

SUMMARY

Your product brings your retail business to life. It is the element that customers can touch and feel. It is the element that can be turned into cash. Cash that will allow you to go and do great things both within and outside your business.

I cannot tell you what product to buy. You are the expert, so only you can do that. The power of this chapter is to use that product to make as much money as possible.

You need it to have purpose. There needs to be a strategy to what that product is doing. That strategy needs to complement your brand and be relevant to your customers. Can you see why and how the Product pillar sits alongside the Customer and Brand pillars?

Use the Product pillar to create a strategy for your range. Think about the Product Life Cycle and start planning the next season or selling window of your business. Having seasonal or quarterly campaigns will add a focus to what you are doing. It will keep your people challenged and interested in what they are doing day-to-day. It will keep your customers engaged and eager to see what you will do next. It will provide a focus to your marketing and storytelling.

As you build that product range, watch your margin carefully. Negotiate for everything because everyone is depending on you to do so. When you've finished negotiating, go back and ask for some more. You will never regret it. Remember, in negotiation, nothing is agreed until everything is agreed.

Watching your margin will ensure you extract cash from product. Knowing which product is selling, what needs pushing, and ensuring your people know which products give you the best margin returns will be critical in your success.

Never lose sight of why you run your business. Your product is your passion and you must allow yourself time to enjoy it. But you're not doing this for a hobby, you're doing this to make money. Lots of money. Your objective now is to become a successful retailer and that means that you need to extract cash from your product.

PILLAR 4: PEOPLE

"Culture eats strategy for breakfast" is a well-known quote from management consultant and author, Peter Drucker. He doesn't mean that strategy is unimportant, but that a powerful and empowering culture is a more certain path to business success. You will know plenty of other anecdotes, "People work for people, not organisations", or "I didn't leave my job, I left my boss."

What is certain is that if you research successful businesses and look at interviews with long-standing and successful teams, they all will say that they enjoyed their work, they knew what their strategic purpose was day-to-day, and that everyone was aligned behind the same goals and objective. I will add to this that they were given the tools to do their jobs well.

You'll recall from the independent retailer survey results that one of the top three outcomes was "My sales staff are not good enough." This theme came through again and again as I talked to independent retailers. If you run the company, then you are the only person who can change this. Either you have recruited the wrong type of people, or you haven't trained them in what it is they should be doing, or you are not rewarding them for what they do. Rewards certainly do not need to be financial. We can assume that everyone would like to be paid more, but after pay, having fun is the most important thing you can give your people.

As I said in the introduction to Part 2, you can't do this on your own. People and great teams are one of the most important assets you can have in your business. As we know from the Brand pillar, people and brand are intertwined. As the face of your business they represent your brand; let's take this a stage further and agree that the type of people you employ will shape the brand in the eyes of your customers.

This is retail and it's a selling environment. You need to find the best possible people, and then you need to nurture them to become superb in whatever role you have identified for them. Very clearly, you need to set out your expectations for that role and regularly check in to ensure those expectations are being met and exceeded. You need to help your people to be the best they can be.

The People pillar is broken down into three core parts; you will find these the easiest to remember from the outset: Recruit, Retain, and Reward. By the end of the chapter you will have a strategy for hiring your shop floor teams, and you will know how to retain them and turn them into a phenomenal asset who will not want to leave your business.

1. RECRUIT

THE ROLE OF THE BUSINESS OWNER

Whether you are the founder or the current leader of the business you need to be comfortable with knowing that you are the magnetic north of your business. Every decision in the end will defer to you. The spirit of the business will be shaped and moulded by you.

Will you take every decision? No. However, your job is to provide the riverbanks within which your people know what decisions to take. You need to be clear on what is allowable and what needs to be referred to someone else to decide. Imagine how frustrating your life will be if you don't set those riverbanks. You would never do anything other than take decisions.

You need to set the rules. Michael E. Gerber, the author of *The E-Myth,* refers to it as a game. You create the rules of the game, and you can change and should change the rules of the game. You can remove someone from the game if they are not playing by the rules. And, as with any game, there needs to be a winner and you should make sure that there are winners and that there are those that didn't win.

By setting the boundaries and by clearly identifying the strategy your business will follow, you will continue to elevate yourself as the key figure that everyone can pull behind, and you will provide clarity to your teams about the objectives they are trying to achieve.

I want you to feel inspired to lead your teams. I truly hope that this book reignites passion for business owners to lead great retail enterprises that do good for their communities, their customers, and their people. If you understand that you can set the tone for every customer interaction that your business has, and that you can shape that experience, then you will take the principles in this chapter very seriously.

You can't do this on your own. You need great people alongside you.

THE MYTH OF RETAIL

A widely held belief is that retail attracts the most unskilled staff. It is relatively easy to find an entry level job in retail. There are so many opportunities and the workforce can be transient as a result. Retailers everywhere focus on filling staffing gaps and then don't ensure that the new employee is ready to succeed.

It takes time to be brilliant at what you do, so right from the off you need to help your people become brilliant. The flip side of the argument is that your people could leave, so for that reason it is far too often the case that investment is not made in the most junior employees in retail. Consequently, they don't enjoy their roles, they are unable to make the best of it, and they look for opportunities elsewhere.

Why do these multi-million-pound businesses accept this? There is an oft-quoted exchange between the sales director and the finance director:

Sales Director: "I want some money to invest in training our sales teams."

Finance Director: "What if we train these staff up and they leave?"

Sales Director: "What if we don't train them and they stay?"

You know where I stand on this. You can't take any chances and hope that your next employee is a gem. You need to polish them and turn them into a shining gold nugget yourself. In fact, you need to set up a system to do this repeatedly.

THE RETAIL LADDER

Whilst many people do leave retail after a short stint on the shop floor, the career opportunities in retail are in fact far greater than in many other industries. For those who want to stick with it, there is a very clear ladder that can be climbed in a multitude of directions leading to a wonderful and fulfilling career. For a sales assistant who shows commitment and loyalty, they can very quickly be given a job as a supervisor, in charge of a section of the shop floor. This may not be reflected in a pay rise but in terms of extra responsibility. Before long they are being asked to be a key holder or to do the cashing up at night. Soon an opportunity arises to be a floor manager or an assistant manager in a smaller store elsewhere. After a while they become assistant manager in a bigger store. Soon they are identified as a future store manager and run their first standalone shop. I've seen people make the leap from sales assistant to store manager in less than two years and been highly capable in each role along the way.

You can take a retail career in many directions. The creative ones may end up in design or visual merchandising, some may see a career in marketing or buying, or others with a flair for the detail could become merchandisers. All merchandisers should have spent some time on the shop floor to understand the intricacies of the role.

It is nearly always the case that a retail director or operations director can tell a story of how they started out serving their first customers with a weekend job in a bar or store.

When you're taking on a new starter to the industry, be sure to tell them where their career could go.

ROLE DESCRIPTION AND JOB ADVERT

Before you take a sales assistant on, be sure you know precisely what the role involves. Ideally, you have done the role yourself first so can write down in explicit detail what is required, when, and what the result of doing the role well will be. If you can't do this then either you don't need the role, or you haven't considered it fully.

Once you know what role you are looking to fill, start recruiting. Place an advert. Here's what has worked for me before. Firstly, make sure the style of your advert is in keeping with your brand principles, that it is consistent with your logos and fonts, and the tone of voice reflects who you are. Secondly, make sure when you read it you would want to work there. Too many job adverts focus on the mundane parts of the job. You need this to excite and inspire. Imagine it has been produced by the marketing team and not the HR team. If you are asking for a CV or covering letter, then say briefly what you want to see included. Too many CVs are full of hot air. The things that interest me the most tend to be the extra-curricular stuff like they have a young family, or they like mountain climbing. I'm not that interested in them achieving a 98% mystery shop result in their last job. Finally, say when the role will be filled and how to send in applications. I would keep it short and snappy and leave a sense of intrigue about the role.

"Do you want to meet great people, have bucket loads of fun, and be rewarded for doing a great job? We are not looking for sales assistants, but customer service gurus, people that will love our customers as much as we do. If you think that's you then drop us a really short CV and a letter about yourself to xxxx by xxxx."

You can answer their questions when you meet them, so don't try to answer everything in the advert.

RECRUITING THE RIGHT PEOPLE

Group recruitment evenings are an innovative alternative to the standard, one-to-one interview process. You want to aim to have at least five people in the room. My previous business hosted a similar event where food and drink were served to the candidates whilst our most on brand people circulated amongst them.

Every candidate had to stand up and tell us about themselves in front of the group; they had to role play selling something, and they had to have a short chat with each of our existing team members who were there on the night. We quickly saw who had the confidence to be one of our people. This is business and you can't have shrinking violets, but also, we could weed out the loud mouths in the group as well. It was far better than a structured face-to-face interview. Remember, recruit behaviour over ability. You can teach ability.

I highly recommend this approach and have used it in my own brands. When you invite people to the interview, make clear what they will be doing: that there will be a group and you will be looking to see who stands out.

The other obvious advantage to this style of evening is that it takes less time than doing multiple interviews. You don't have to be polite asking questions to someone you made your mind up about the moment they walked in.

ONBOARDING PLAN FROM APPOINTMENT, TO WELCOME LETTER, TO INDUCTION PACK

Once you've appointed a new team member you need to accelerate their enthusiasm for the brand. Even the unsuccessful candidates need looking after. A well-worded letter of regret is going to keep them positive about your business. Perhaps you could include a discount off their next shop either online or in-store. Be careful to ensure it's a gesture of goodwill and doesn't come across as insulting.

New starters will need managing. Send them a letter with their contract. Your letter should welcome them to the brand, give them advice on what your brand does, and who your customers are. Once they are at their most enthusiastic you can use this time to start bringing them up to speed on what you do.

Once you bring a new starter in you must ensure they fully understand what they are being asked to do. Induct your people into every role.

Run through the job description in detail with the new starter, bring it to life, pause and ask questions to check it is fully understood. Finally, check they still want the job. It really is crucial that new starters are given the tools to succeed from the outset. Can you see why it is so critical to have carefully considered the intricacies of the role you want them to do? If you are not crystal clear about what they need to do to succeed, then what hope do they have?

As you build your business towards new levels of maturity you should create assets that make your life simpler as you go. A document for onboarding new employees, once complete, will be used again and again. Include a tick list of things you will run through with every new starter.

Ask them to tick it off with you. This document's an agreement between both sides that you have explained and agreed what the role entails. You can add to this document as you go. Don't see creating it as onerous, but as the introduction of a system that will make your life simpler in the long run.

THE CONTRACT

The contract of employment will need necessary legalese to set out what is expected and what is not acceptable. There are employment contracts available online, but this is an area where I would seek professional legal advice as soon as you can afford to do so. As with your induction pack, it's another asset that your business will benefit from in the long run.

Use the contract not just as a piece of paper but a set of expectations. It should set out the rules of the game. You can add to it with letters of variation as the game changes or new roles are taken on.

SUMMARY

People spend far too much of their life working for it to be anything other than time well spent. When you bring people into your business you have a responsibility to ensure that they can fulfil and exceed their own expectations. The good news is that it pays back.

The more tools you can give them to be successful, the more successful they will be.

Selecting the right people for your business is dependent on your being clear about what it is they are required to do, and ensuring they fully understand the role they are being asked to do, and how to be successful in doing it.

You can use the onboarding process from job advert, to recruitment event, to appointment and induction as a way of building your brand. You will build assets as you go that add value to the greater strength of your business, but also you can use the process as a way of indoctrinating your new starters into the way your brand looks and feels.

EXERCISE

Draw up a detailed job description for each role in your business.
Draw up a job advert that reflects your brand.
Plan a recruitment evening that will bring out the best qualities of your candidates.
Create an onboarding document with a tick box list for you and your new starter to work through during their induction.

2. RETAIN

TRAINING

Working with younger shop floor staff is hugely rewarding. They are like sponges, soaking up the information you teach them. They are used to learning and being taught so approach it in the right frame of mind. Sometimes older sales assistants can be less receptive to learning new approaches. I remember struggling with a pair of ladies who had worked on beauty counters on Oxford Street 30 years before and told me there was nothing they didn't know about selling. When I mentioned Facebook, they paused and said, "Do you really think that's going to be a thing? I mean, why on earth would you want to share everything you are doing on the internet?" This was in 2019.

Your success will sit firmly on the shoulders of your people. The only way they are going to be successful is to show them how. Please, understand that regular and well-planned training on Customer, Brand, Product, and Sales is imperative to retail success.

You need to set out when people first join that there will be regular training sessions. "You will be trained every week at an agreed time. It's compulsory. It's part of your contract for working here that you attend training."

TRAINING PROGRAMME

Apple train their staff for an hour every day. High street banks open an hour later one day a week for staff training. You can't ignore training so make time for it. You will never regret developing your staff to be better at their jobs. Keep in mind that your suppliers may well have a budget for training, so ask them if they will provide it.

I would focus the training around the pillars of Customer, Brand, Product, and Sales. It needs to be relevant and thought through in advance. You could take a few pages from this book and make the topic applicable to your business. Whatever you do, test the learning. Follow up the next day or later, on the shop floor. If you are teaching a new selling technique, encourage everyone to go and practise it that day and the next day. It will be pointless if habits are not formed and the training is forgotten within a few days.

If you're daunted by training, then take the time to plan it. Save your training sessions afterwards so you can reuse them on a rotation as necessary. As a structure I find the four Ts a useful rule of thumb.

1. **Tell them what they are going to learn**
2. **Teach them**
3. **Tell them what they have just learned**
4. **Test the learning**

Share the learning around. You know from your regular reviews where the skills sit in your business. Ask those with the skills to take the next week's training session. This has an added benefit for the teacher. The best way to learn is by teaching. They may be instinctively good at something, but teaching it forces people to understand the principles behind the subject.

PEOPLE SURVEYS, LISTENING, AND LEARNING

Ask your staff what would make their jobs easier. Pret A Manger worked with their staff and a footwear manufacturer to design a shoe that would keep them comfortable on their feet all day. The staff can buy this shoe at a heavily discounted price. Listen to your people and help find ways for them to be brilliant at their jobs.

If you do decide to do a people survey you can utilise a platform like Survey Monkey. I would ensure that you ask similar questions each year or bi-annually to ensure you are tracking progress. Share the results of people surveys and commit to working to improve areas that are lacking.

Whatever you do, make sure you listen and learn. Your people are giving you invaluable feedback that will enhance your business. It may not be possible to give people everything they ask for, but try to explain the reasons why not. Finally, make sure you really highlight the things you have acted on. "You said, we did."

STRATEGY FOR REVIEWS AND TOUCH POINTS

Check back regularly on your employees. Measure how well they are doing and share the results of this with them. The reason teachers set tests and exams is to measure learning. The only way you can see how well your people have taken on board what you have taught them is to test the learning. This doesn't need to be an exam, although an online questionnaire is easy to set up and can be rolled out quickly.

More important is that you set time aside with individuals to see how they are finding the role they have been given. Retrieve the job description and onboarding checklist and agree together how well each aspect of the role is being conducted.

Regular reviews are good practice and should be encouraged. Irregular reviews tend to be counterproductive. Twice a year is too infrequent to sit down and have a considered conversation. Too much time has built up. Monthly or bi-monthly reviews will take the pressure off both employee and manager, and will ensure you know what motivates your people. How else will you spot the future potential of your team if you don't take the time to know what interests them? The more they open up to you, the more trust you will build and the better relationship you can have.

As your business grows you will need to identify the talent in your team to fill new roles.

There are many tactics and strategies in this book. You can't expect to deliver them all yourself, so it's far better to identify the talent in your team that can take on different roles and responsibilities in building your business. It is through the regular touch points with your employees that you can find the skills and talents that will help you implement your strategy to achieve your objective.

CULTURE

The success Jack Wills enjoyed in its first 10–12 years was in a large part down to the environment. It's nonsense to suggest we had brilliant people; we had ordinary people who were encouraged to be themselves and given the environment to grow and express themselves. Create the environment, stoke it with regularly organised fun, and engage the team on what's important to them. Then work to deliver that. The upshot is you attract top people with the right mindset to add to and enhance your culture. Indulge them to do just that.

Organised fun in and out of work will build team camaraderie. Allow it to happen and encourage it to. Building a culture of enjoyment with work will reap rewards in the long run.

SHARE THE OBJECTIVE AND THE STRATEGY

I've mentioned how *The E-Myth* refers to the management of people as a game. A game with rules and winners. To be a winner you need to know the rules of the game and how to win. Show your people where the finish line is or when the game will end. Have a target and make sure everyone knows when that needs to be reached or how well you've done in reaching the target. Who did well? Who needs to work harder?

To do this you need to share the objective and the strategy for achieving it. Here's the objective I suggested at the start of Part 2: *"My objective is to become a successful retailer, to create as much profit in my business as possible, so that I can do great things for my family and make a real change in the world."* You may have a revised objective for your team but whatever you do, tell them what the objective is, what it is you want them to achieve, and the way you want them to achieve it.

You need them to have bought into the plan. Give clear direction, give clear communication, and ensure it's understood; if it's not, revisit it.

SUMMARY

People want to do well. It's a matter of pride and self-esteem to want to do a good job and do a good job well.

To ensure your employees are operating at their best, make sure they are clear as to what their job is. Check in regularly that they are doing it as you expected and in doing so ask if there is a better way of doing it. A new set of eyes on a task is invaluable.

You will know which parts of your business are strongest, and which of the pillars in this book need more attention. Through training your people, you can focus on the areas of weakness and explore a strategy to correct that imbalance. If you need everyone to spend time understanding your customers, then a training session is the place.

Make sure that people are happy at work. Your regular surveys and conversations with the team can draw this out. If the culture is not right, then you must address it fast. You invest so much time and money in your people, so you need to nurture them, understand their skills and ambitions, and harness that talent and give it the space to be brilliant. You can't afford to let good talent leave. Stay close to them, understand their motivations, and then reward them for being brilliant.

EXERCISE

Organise fun or ask one of your team to.
Create a people survey.

Identify areas of weakness in your business and arrange a training session to address them.

3. REWARD

Too often salespeople are not rewarded for their success. If the best paid employee in your business was a sales assistant who deservedly earned fantastic commissions, would that be a bad thing? If someone is successful in your business, then you will be the biggest beneficiary.

PAY

Typically, retail doesn't pay well at the bottom rungs of the ladder. The sense being that it is unskilled work which doesn't require training to do. Well, I hope by now we have disproved that point. Therefore, retail must be skilled work that just doesn't pay well. To be honest, that doesn't sit well with me either.

You need to decide where you sit on this one. How much you pay is up to you, but know that rewarding your team for being successful will help you retain the talent you have carefully nurtured.

As a minimum you should check, annually, how much other businesses in your local area are paying. This benchmarking exercise will ensure you are not too high or too low.

CREATE A PERFOMANCE-RELATED BONUS

In a sales environment, a performance-related bonus is absolutely the right way to go. You need to dangle the carrot of more cash in front of your sales teams, either individually or as a group, but ideally both.

You need to decide what you will link your bonus to. In the next chapter on Sales you will find the section "Everything measured improves". There are multiple metrics in here that capture the performance of your business. Any one of these or a combination of a few will be a good place to start.

Whatever happens, the bonus must be linked to a metric that grows your business. Increasing ATV is one, increasing transactions another, increasing footfall another.

Whatever you choose, make sure that after all the costs are accounted for your business is still better off. I know of a call centre that offered a bonus linked to top-line sales. Everyone successfully flogged a low margin product which ultimately didn't make the business any better off. They quickly stopped that bonus.

CALCULATE WHAT YOU CAN AFFORD TO GIVE AWAY IN AN ATTRACTIVE BONUS

If sales in a store went up by £100,000 over a period and your profit margin was 10% then you know you can't give away a bonus of £10,000. But would you be happy to give away £1,000? Seems reasonable. What if that happened every quarter of the year? Both you and the employee would be pleased with the results.

Most bonus packages in retail pay up to 10% of salary. I have seen 20% and 25% bonus pots. There are very stretching targets linked to these, as there should be. But the best people do achieve them.

A further 10% a year on top of salary is a minimum and whilst the target should be achievable, it must be beneficial to your business. Consider structuring a bonus up to 25% for achieving stretched targets; this will be mutually very beneficial.

BONUS IS GIVEN THROUGHOUT THE YEAR, NOT ONCE A YEAR

Keep it interesting. If you set a quarterly target and after three weeks it's clear they can't achieve it, then the incentive and momentum is gone. Cash is king and people want to see it in their pay packets. You'll be impressed by how motivated your people will be to hit those sales targets.

Having an annual bonus is not ideal in a sales environment. It does have merit for head office staff as they manage performance over a longer period and are unable to influence income performance in the same way a sales team can.

For sales teams, build in regular bonus periods. Monthly or quarterly as a minimum. You could still have an overall bonus for the full 12 months as well. If you decide that a 10% bonus can be achieved over a year, then dividing that up over 4 quarters at 2.5% each is a sensible strategy. Nothing worse than the whole year being ruined by one bad quarter due to too much snow or some badly placed roadworks.

BONUS IS USED AS A TOOL FOR DRIVING RETAIL SUCCESS

The bonus should be achievable if you consistently worked hard. I achieved my bonus one quarter as a regional manager by hitting a sales target of many millions of pounds with about £2,000 to spare. During the final weekend of that quarter I had store managers pulling together for me who knew their own bonus situation was already decided. I had promised I would reward them, as I needed them to still work hard. There were drinks all round to celebrate and a night out on me.

Create the environment and they will come through for you. Set the targets, show how to achieve them through explaining the rules of the bonus and giving good training, and then recognise and reward. Stick to this and your business will be rewarded in return.

One last word on bonus. Celebrate success. If you're in charge and one of your team has achieved their bonus, then make a point of congratulating them. Either a letter or a phone call or an announcement in a company-wide email. They have worked for this and the whole business has benefitted. They should be widely praised.

MONEY ISN'T EVERYTHING

Remember, financial remuneration is not the only reward you can offer. A wide-reaching employee survey in the food and beverage sector showed that after money, the most important reason for coming to work was fun. A good culture and team ethic on the shop floor will be picked up by your customers, so they will know if there's a happy vibe in your stores.

CELEBRATING SUCCESS

When I have had great teams and great cultures there were never any pay complaints. When I wanted a team to work through the night, I had a string of volunteers. Why? We were all loving what we were doing and bought into the objective. We were proud to say, "I did that."

People like to be thanked for doing a good job and at Jack Wills we arranged weekends away for the best performing managers, including skiing weekends in France. It was a great incentive for our people, as the managers desperately wanted to go and worked hard to be selected. From a brand perspective it was positive as long skiing weekends were what our customers were enjoying, and we wanted them to experience that first-hand. As you can imagine, great bonds were built, stories were told, and it ensured our best, most deserving people wanted to stay and work hard for us.

ORGANISE FUN

Regularly organise fun or nominate someone else to organise fun as part of their role. Whether it's a night out on the town with a few drinks or on the shop floor activities that drive competition and conversation, you need to ensure that your people can build relationships with you and each other that are not entirely based on work.

The ski trip worked for Jack Wills, but it doesn't need to be a big expensive cost. Regular offsite team events are a necessity, not a good idea for some other time. There must be some upsides to the day-to-day routines. Where possible, combine work and fun. Use an offsite event to state your objectives and remind people of the strategy. Reset the rules of the game at an offsite event, introduce a new bonus or reward system. Then, once you've rallied the troops behind the objective, go and have a few drinks to celebrate all the hard work that has gone in up to now.

RECOGNITION

"People don't leave bad jobs, they leave bad bosses." People like to be told they have done a good job or worked hard. It is so simple to recognise good work and great results.

Some staff don't need an arm around the shoulder, others do. You should pay attention to what motivates different team members. There are some who like to grumble about how hard they work. Tell them that you know they work hard, that you rely on them because they are dependable and hardworking. The louder ones will tell everyone how well they are doing and what bonus they achieved. The quieter ones will achieve it in their own way. Don't forget to compliment them even if they don't overtly seek it out.

STAFF DISCOUNTS

There's often a very good reason that someone applies to work in your store. Hopefully it's because they share your passion for what you do. A staff discount scheme is a good way of rewarding them. You may choose to make some things unavailable for staff to buy at a discount, particularly if it's a limited edition item. You should also limit how much they can buy so you don't lose too much great stock for a low margin.

There should be perks for working for you and a staff discount is one of them.

MORE HOURS

Give a smaller number of people more hours and you will spend less on recruitment and invest in retention. People need to pay their bills. Train your people to be great at what they do, and then if they want to work more hours you should encourage them to do so. It's far better they do it than taking on someone new who needs training to do so.

PROMOTION

Within the career ladder you can add in more responsibility. This shows that people are trusted, and it tells other employees that someone is trusted and they in turn will feel valued. Feeling valued goes a long way to fuelling loyalty.

Internal promotion is nearly always the best tack. Of course, that employee doesn't have experience at the role they are moving to, but they understand your organisation, objectives and company culture far better than a new starter. And you know what they are capable of.

You may have to catch them every now and again, but if you show them the riverbanks they can work within and give them the latitude to relax into the role, you will see them thrive.

SUMMARY

There is no excuse for your sales staff to not be good enough. To achieve the dreams you have for your business and for yourself you need your people to be excellent.

People management could take up all your time. The sooner you create systems for bringing them on board efficiently, training them in understanding your Customers and your Brand, and knowing all about your Product and how to sell it, the easier your job will be and the more successful you will be.

It is through systems that you can shape your people to be a powerful asset for you.

You can't do this on your own, so you need to harness the talent of others. Go and find them, train them to be outstanding, recognise their achievements, and reward their success.

The best rewards work both ways. If someone goes above and beyond for your business, then ensure they are recognised and rewarded. The two of you should be sharing in their success. You have worked hard to find them and nurture them and you deserve to benefit from all that effort. But you do need to keep them sweet.

EXERCISE

Create a bonus structure.
Identify someone in your team to oversee organising nights out.
Who deserves recognition for a great piece of work?

PILLAR 5: SALES

Well done, it's now time to take some cash. The first four pillars, Customer, Brand, Product, and People have all been essential in making it possible to take money. And, with these pillars in place, you will take lots of money. But you've come too far to not take the last part as seriously as the first four.

For many retail entrepreneurs the taking of money is why they started. They don't have the same passion for their product that others do; it's more likely they saw an opportunity to make some money. If that's you then surround yourself with people who can build the Brand and understand the Customers and the Product. These eulogists and enthusiasts will help you.

Whatever your reasons for running your business, you are in it primarily for the making of money.

There are three parts to the Sales pillar: Train, Sell, and Measure. Training follows on from the People pillar and investigates techniques that will work in your store to grow ATV throughout the customers' touchpoints as they make a transaction. Sell is broken down into five parts that create the ideal selling environment. Measure encourages you to take the data that is abundant in your business and use it to continuously achieve greater success.

1. TRAIN

I'm staggered by this, but it's true. Whenever I ask salespeople how much time has been spent training them in selling skills, it's nearly always the lowest compared to using the till, cashing up, dressing the window or stocking the shelves. It does make me wonder why they are called salespeople.

The base expectation of a sales assistant is that they can sell. If they have the right character, and you will have determined that through the People pillar, then with your Customer identified, your Brand credentials established, and your awesome Product working hard for you, the Sales will follow. You have worked so hard to bring a customer into your store; you can't throw it away now with people who are not trained to be brilliant.

For many, Roger Federer is the best tennis player of all time; he has had a coach throughout his career.

In the People pillar I encouraged you to set time aside every week for training. You need to weight this training towards sales skills. Becoming good at selling, much like becoming a champion tennis player, takes time and practice.

It will not go perfectly the first time, but it will improve the more you do it. You need to be ready to challenge yourself to sell well and to train your team to sell well.

During Christmas, when shops are busy, are your staff selling well or are they just processing transactions for a customer who is in the right frame of mind for shopping? Can you say with hand on heart that you are squeezing as much cash out of every customer who crosses the threshold of your stores? That is the goal. With each customer your team has a sales conversation with, you need to ensure that the customer leaves with as much of your product as they can carry.

You need to train your people and give them the tools to succeed. Tools that will give them confidence. There are some excellent books on selling; one I highly recommend is *You Are The Difference* by Alf Dunbar. What I will do here is give a few tips I have used myself and I know are successful and are being used by many successful retailers.

MOOD AND ATMOSPHERE

Alf Dunbar talks about being in the right mood for selling. You want the atmosphere in your stores to be one of positivity. Is the music volume right? Is the store warm or cool enough?

Your people need to be in the right frame of mind to sell. If they have been soaked waiting for the bus in the rain and turn up in a bad mood, then that's not going to put them in the right place to serve customers. At Selfridges there is a compulsory 15 minute briefing before the start of every shift for all sales people. This is the chance to warm everyone up for a day of great selling ahead. Raise the mood and cheer up your teams; you have some great customers coming in today and you're going to show them your fabulous product.

GREETING THE CUSTOMERS

There is nothing worse for a customer than walking into an empty, quiet shop with sales assistants standing with their hands by their sides waiting to pounce. It is so intimidating no wonder customers walk out as quickly as possible. The music volume can help you here, as it will make the store feel less empty.

Never let people stand behind the till or cash desk unless they are processing a transaction. There should be a trap door behind the cash desk that your people will fall through if they are standing there without a customer to talk to. I'm only half joking here. The cash desk creates a barrier between you and the customers which you want to remove. You should avoid creating barriers unless you absolutely need to.

To diminish the intimidation for customers as they enter, you want your team to be busy. Ideally, they are replenishing or tidying shelves or generally tasking while remaining alert to customers entering the store. It will reassure the customers that they are not about to be pounced on.

Your busy sales staff should acknowledge someone a few seconds after they have arrived. Never, ever ask a question. Always make a statement.

Don't say, "Hi, how are you today?" or "Is there anything I can help you with" or "Is there anything you are looking for?" Even in a bar you should avoid saying "What would you like?"

You must avoid questions.

Remember the first few interactions with your neighbour we talked about in the Brand pillar? When you meet someone new or go somewhere new your first reactions will be primitive. Your senses are heightened and intuitively your mind is led by fight or flight. Your job in making the greeting statement is to reassure the customers that you have seen them, made them aware that you don't sound like a scary person, and that you are not going to attack them. Therefore, you can't ask a question. They are already processing multiple senses, so the last thing they need is to be put under pressure and think they are about to be sold to.

Ever wondered why some retailers have incredibly attractive people working by the front door? Abercrombie and Fitch used to take it a stage further, employing young men with their tops off displaying wash board stomachs to stand at the front door and greet their customers. It doesn't take much to deduce that their customers are mainly young girls. Equally, as the greeter says "Welcome to Abercrombie and Fitch" he can then be the first person to field a question from the customers. They may just want immediate directions to a department or certain product. Employing someone just to stand and greet is expensive and might need to wait a little while, but, positioning attractive salespeople by the front door is money well spent.

Greeting statements just need to be short. "Hi there" will do. "Just shout if you need anything" could be used if you know the customer has been in a while, or perhaps in a traditional butcher or baker setting with a counter in place. Make the greeting statement without stopping what you are doing, look at them, hold their eye contact, but keep busying yourself. You are inviting them to make the next move when they are ready.

REASSURE THE CUSTOMERS' THINKING

Avoiding asking questions is important, as you want the customers to start the questioning rather than you, yourself. One simple technique we employed in my clothing brands was to go and re-stock a shelf near a customer and then make a positive reassuring statement about the clothes the customer was looking at: "I love those shirts." Or, "That shirt was our best seller last week." Or, "I've bought one of those." Quite simply we are telling the customer they have good taste and reassuring them that they are right to pause by this garment. Other customers have done so and they are in good company. They are not alone in thinking this is good.

GROW THE SALE

The purpose of the reassuring statement is to draw the customers into a conversation if they are ready. The job of the sales assistant is to find out what the customers are looking for, listen for signals, and then fulfil their needs and wants.

This is where all their product training needs to come out. When you know what a customer is looking for, and this means listening to them first, then you can introduce items for them. Once they have started buying, keep introducing new products for them until they stop. Alf Dunbar recommends asking "Is there anything else you need?" The key to this is the word 'need'. Not, 'want', 'like', 'looking for'. It must be 'need'. Need brings out a different response. You might say at Christmas, "Is there anyone else you need to buy for?" Alf's advice is to keep asking the need question until they stop shopping.

INCREASE ATV – THE MCDONALD'S THEORY

Once you have a customer shopping with you, you need them to spend as much money as possible. We know how important it is to grow ATV from when we studied "The Science of Retail" chapter at the end of Part 1. By introducing more and more items, you will grow the ATV.

One simple technique you can start today is something I call the McDonald's Theory. Every time you order a burger at McDonald's, the staff will come back with the sentence, "Do you want French fries with that?" They are all trained to say it. What is your equivalent of the French fries?

Try out this exercise: during quiet periods ask your people to pick up any item in your stores and say what they would 'up sell' with it if a customer brought it to the till. Burger = fries; shirt = tie; sandwich = drink; plant = watering can. Keep your team practising this all the time and then watch them introduce these additional items to the customers.

Everything you sell should have something that complements it further. Your people need to be relaxed and practised at the McDonald's Theory. Keep introducing complementary items again and again until the customer has finished shopping.

INCREASE ATV – BUNDLING

Meal deals are a brilliant example of growing ATV. Rather than just buying a sandwich, the customers walk out with a drink and a chocolate bar as well. Instead of paying £2.99 they spent £3.99. ATV just went up by 33%.

Look at your product and your best and most frequent sellers. What else do people buy with these items? Can you produce a bundle that will encourage more of your customers to spend more cash when they come in to buy a best seller?

It works well online. You will often see an image pop up next to something after you have added it to your basket, such as: "Customers who bought this item also bought this."

CLOSE THE SALE

Everything in this book, and everything you have worked for has led to this moment. You are about to take some actual money. You have done all the hard work identifying your Customer, building a Brand that will appeal to them, creating a beautiful, brilliant Product that they need, and training your People to be outstanding at epitomising your customers, representing your brand, and showcasing your product. Now is the time to close that sale.

You need to ask for the sale. Find a way that you are comfortable with and be brave. The more you do it the more you will become confident in it and eventually forget what you are doing.

"Shall I put that in a bag for you?"

"Would you like to take these?"

"Shall I take these over to the till for you?"

"Is there anything else you need me to tell you about this product?"

Whatever is right for your store and brand is what you need to work on. The good news is that in most environments your brand and product correctly targeted at the right customers will have pre-sold your product already. The customers will have made their minds up already that they are going to be making a transaction today. What you and your people are doing is ensuring they buy as many of your products as possible and that by explaining the qualities of each product, the customers will enjoy them as much as possible. This is important as it breeds likeability and trust in your product. You have worked hard to win these customers and now you want them to come back again and again.

CAPTURE THEIR DATA

Make sure that you can stay in touch with them. As you close the sale ask if they would like to receive special promotions from you. Introduce your loyalty card. Say that there are events coming up for certain customers, and would they like to hear about it. Suggest they follow you on Instagram or Facebook. You want them to give you as many details as possible: email address, home address, phone number, birthday. Whatever is relevant to your business that you can create a marketing technique around will be valuable.

As you are gathering their data, explain more of the benefits that you can share with them in exchange for the data. They will be the first to hear about the end of season sale or when new stock arrives.

Data is an asset and you need to continuously grow this asset. Assets have value, so keep investing in your customer database asset by adding contact details to it and the value you can extract will grow as well.

SUMMARY

Your people need to be given the tools to sell well. For a new employee on the shop floor those first interactions with a real customer are nerve-racking; there is so much to remember. You need to coach them through it. Listen to their interaction and give them feedback afterwards. Tell them what they did well, and tell them what they should try doing next time. Slowly introduce new techniques. You are going to reward your team for selling well and the better they do the better you do. Be certain they have all the tools they can possibly have to succeed.

EXERCISE

Book in a sales training session.
Arrange briefings before each shift starts for every member of the team.
Practise the McDonald's Theory with your people.

2. SELL

Having trained your people so they are ready to make you lots of money, you need to ensure the selling environment is set up to make the buying and selling process as easy as possible.

A lot of the work is done; you have been marketing and creating a brand that resonates with your specific customers. Now you need to take as much money as possible and ensure your hard won customers come back again and again. Remember the Science of Retail; you need to grow ATV and transactions and penetration.

The middle part of the Sales pillar is to 'sell'. You want to be making as much money as often as possible.

There are five steps to creating the ideal 'sell' environment:

I.   **Pre-awareness**
II. **Visual merchandising**
III. **Promotions**
IV. **Your people**
V.   **Loyalty**

I.   PRE-AWARENESS

The concept of "Build it and they will come" is nonsense. When I launched one of my clothing brands, we had a launch party every Thursday evening for the first month. Week one we invited the media; week two was for local residents – quite simply we put a note through the door of about a hundred houses and flats; week three was for our friends and family who were desperate to see the business do well; finally in week four we had a party and invited everyone who had made a purchase in the first few weeks. We told everyone it was a chance to meet them properly and say thank you for their support. The truth was we just needed cash. But it worked and by the end of it we had started a new tribe of followers. The booze was provided on a sale or return basis at a heavy discount by a local off-licence in return for us promoting them during the events.

When we were selling our clothing range at multiple outdoor events all over the country, we ensured we collected the email addresses of our customers whenever they came into our store. We noted down which event they were collected at and then a week before the same event the following year we sent them an email inviting them to come and enjoy a glass of champagne in the store. They just had to bring a copy of the email or show it on their phone. Once they had the champagne in hand and we were chatting away we would deliver some more value for being one of our customers; they could enjoy a discount if they spent over £50 today. This discount was extra added value for being our customer. The time-limited pressure of the offer ensured that the next sale was made immediately. The £50 threshold ensured our ATV was growing.

When you truly know your customers and they know your brand then you will have customers queuing up to shop with you. Remember the mantra, "People attract people." It's known by psychologists as social proof. If people see a busy restaurant, they are more likely to queue up to go in then go to an empty restaurant next door.

With your Customer identified and your Brand tailored towards them, the marketing you do should ensure that they are warmed up to making a purchase. Now you need to convert them into a customer.

II. VISUAL MERCHANDISING – THE LOOK AND FEEL OF YOUR STORE

When I joined Selfridges, I was swamped by merchandisers and visual merchandisers. I didn't know who did what. Merchandisers, as described in the Product pillar, manage the stock from a margin perspective. They ensure the right amount of stock is sold at the right price in the right place.

Visual merchandisers are creatives. They make a store look and feel great. They will take the stock package that the merchandiser has selected for the store and display it, so it looks attractive and so that customers want to touch it. They will consider the product display, the lighting, the music, the smells, and how your windows and point of sale signage is utilised.

A well-displayed store will give your customer an impression about the quality of your product and the perception they have of your brand. If they are inspired by the product along with the look and feel of the store, then these positive impressions will make them more likely to buy. Good visual merchandising (VM) will help you convert customers.

SEE IT, BUY IT

A simple mantra for effective VM is "See it, buy it." Wherever there is an in-store display, mannequin or even a poster image of a product, make sure that the product can be found straight away. If there is a mannequin 'look' you are promoting, the items promoted should be on a rail right alongside so the customer can respond to your inspiration straight away. Anything displayed in the window should be found immediately inside the store.

WINDOWS AND HOME PAGE

The window of your offline store and home page of your online store are critical. Think of the Brand Piece Life Cycle in the Brand pillar. For many customers this will be the first touch point they have with your business. It needs to ooze your brand; it needs to shape the customers' expectations of what they will discover inside. Look at the windows and home pages of brands that you admire. Can you see what they have done to make their message stand out and to make their customer go inside to look around? Windows need to be clutter free, seasonally appropriate, and can be used for promoting your business even when the store is closed. Make sure the window is well lit in the evenings when you are closed to attract passing traffic and raise brand awareness. Your carefully selected product and brand message for that moment in time needs to be activating customers to come inside based on what they see in the window or on the home page.

STORE LAYOUT

The most valuable space in your store is the space right by the door. This is where you need your most important sales drivers. Every major department store knows that they make their best sales from beauty products and ladies' handbags. These departments will be right next to the busiest entry points to their stores. They are high footfall, high margin locations, and the VM team know that they need to be well laid out. Anything on the second floor or in the basement of your shop is in a secondary or tertiary position. Make sure that your best sellers are in the best locations.

TOUCHING PRODUCT WILL DRIVE SALES

Manipulating and carefully arranging your space will trigger impulse purchases; it will make your stock easier to see and touch. Once a customer starts to touch the product, they will begin to build an affinity with it and a sense of ownership. Where possible you want your customers to touch as much of your stock as you can allow.

PICK-UP PIECES

I worked with a garden centre whose best-selling product was hand cream. A keen gardener's hands are often in and out of soil, they are outdoors in all temperatures pulling at weeds and sharp thorns in bushes, and constantly being wet and dry. Hand cream was sold for £12 at the till point. If the customer didn't spot it the sales assistant at the till would introduce the product as they were running the rest of the shopping through the till. It was highly effective.

WHSmith have a chocolate bar for £1 by their tills. Without fail, everyone is offered one by the sales assistant. It's a naughty but tasty product at a low price and again effective at driving up ATV.

Your music, the atmosphere, the layout of your store; it will all help put the customer in the right frame of mind for shopping. Well thought through VM will create an environment conducive to shopping.

III. PROMOTIONS

Consumers respond to promotions; they stand out from the other products and are more likely to convert into sales.

If your customer is cash poor, they are more likely to respond to money off promotions rather than percentage off promotions. They only have a certain amount of cash to spend and will be attracted by price.

PROMOTIONAL MATERIAL

Your point of sale (POS) material – typically this is shelf edge signage, promotional posters, and the like – should be clear and do a job for you. If there is a saving or a time-limited period or a gift with purchase, then the messaging needs to make this clear in as simple a way as possible. Show your POS to others before you print it. Make sure everyone understands what the offer is before you show it to the customer. The simpler the message the better.

Finally, make sure that your promotion message is consistent in all your stores, online and offline. Once it's over, don't forget to remove the offer from your points of sale.

SCARCITY AND EXCLUSIVITY

There's nothing like being told you will miss out to make customers buy something. Think of the panic buying that took place ahead of the quarantine lockdowns due to coronavirus. For no logical reason customers were hoarding loo roll. Despite being told there was firstly no clinical reason why you would need more loo roll, and secondly no risk of it running out if everyone just shopped normally, it didn't stop customers taking home more than they could carry. It was driven by a fear of missing out.

It wasn't just loo roll; dried food, tinned food, pasta, baby products all flew off the shelves. It wasn't uncommon to see notes on shelves saying the product would be back in stock in six to eight weeks' time.

You can create scarcity with your products by saying it's a limited edition. When it's gone, it's gone. I've put an expensive limited edition outerwear garment in a catalogue and included in the small print below it, "Limited edition product, only 15 have been made." Simply stating how few were available caused the items to sell within a couple of weeks of them arriving in-store.

The alternative is to promote the product as exclusive. "This is only available in our stores; you can't buy it anywhere else." Alternatively, arrange with a supplier to have it in your store first for four weeks before it goes to other stores.

Ensure you always have selected lines that have very short runs. Promote these preferentially to your best customers first and they will thank you for it. It's ok that some of your customers miss out. They now know that next time they will need to come into your shops much quicker.

Unlike discounted price-led promotions, scarcity and exclusivity can command higher prices.

PUSH LINES

Each week your people should be clear on what they are pushing hardest. This could be a seasonal lamb chop marinated in your special barbecue sauce for a butcher or a new brownie in a coffee shop or an expensive ladies winter coat in a clothes store. There should be POS to go with it, and it should be promoted in a key sales area; everyone needs to know the target you are trying to achieve in pushing it that week.

If you have an item that everyone is focusing on selling, then you will sell more of them. If you have an item that is not selling as well as planned, then putting all your efforts behind it will certainly drive sales. Give your team the tools to succeed and you will make it easy for them to do so.

THE END OF SEASON SALE

For many retailers this is when the big money comes in. You, or your merchandiser if you have one, will have looked at the available product and the current sell through rates and decided what prices to sell at, what the value of the discount is, and what margin you will be left with.

Plan the sale: plan the pricing, the pre-awareness marketing, the store layout, the lines to push, brief the team, take lots of money, and finally capture the customers' data. If this is the busiest time of your year then you need to make sure it's going to be a success and you need to make sure you leverage that success so that you are even more successful in the years ahead. It's going to be busy but that doesn't mean you should stop bringing your brand to life with great in-store activity, or neglecting to ask for customers' contact details. You're on show, the customers have come in. Take full advantage.

IV. YOUR PEOPLE

Your people come through for you now. You've trained them in the Customer, Brand and Product. You've trained them to sell. You will reward them for being great at their job. They know the more they sell, the more they will earn.

BE AN EXPERT; HELP THEM BUY

Your people's role is not so much to sell but to help the customer to buy. They can save the customer time by listening to what they want and finding it for them as quickly as possible or by introducing alternative options. They can explain promotions and how the customer can take advantage of them.

They are experts. Experts in the brand and the product. They have been trained so well that customers look to them for their advice and counsel. Encourage your people to believe that they are experts. This doesn't mean they can be arrogant or flippant, but that the customer will value their opinions and recommendations. When I buy new shoes, I want to know about fit and comfort. When I buy a pork tenderloin, I want to know how to cook it. When I buy a special new brownie, I want to know what ingredients make it special. Encourage your people to be confident in the product that they immerse themselves in every day.

FOUR QUALATIES IN A SALES ASSISTANT

- **Your sales assistants need to be available to help; not busy doing tasks**
- **They need to be knowledgeable experts and able to help customers to buy**
- **They need to be able to build a rapport that will ensure the customer likes and trusts them and wants to come back to your store**
- **They need to listen to the verbal language and read the non-verbal body language of the customer to know when to push their knowledge and when to pull back and be quiet**

Remember, the base expectation of a sales assistant is to sell. This needs training, ongoing support, and rewarding. Do this and your people will be great at their job and they will enjoy it. Your customer will enjoy shopping in your stores, and they will come back again.

V. LOYALTY

In the Customer pillar we looked at the power of building loyalty with your customers. Don't forget, it's far easier to make the next sale to a customer you already have than to one you haven't met yet.

FREE STUFF

I've talked about how giving away free glasses of bubbles helped increase sales in my stores. Many brands use free product to help them build loyalty with their customer base.

Krispy Kreme gives out free doughnuts to celebrate National Doughnut Day which happens the first Friday in June. There's no purchase necessary, you just show up and ask for your free doughnut. It breeds brand loyalty and the likelihood is that the customer will reciprocate with a future purchase. The customer feels like they are having a fair exchange of value.

FOLLOW-ON SALES

Once you have converted a customer, now is the time to keep them warmed up to buying from you. Online customers could be sent a time-limited offer for their next purchase as a thank you. The offer needs to be compelling and the time-limited nature of it will focus them on taking advantage of it whilst your brand is at the front of their mind. In-store the offer could be slipped into the carrier bag before the customer leaves the store.

REFERRALS

Referrals from your customers are incredibly powerful; if you have looked after them well, they are far more likely to tell their friends about you. A good loyalty programme allied with a great customer experience in-store or online will go a long way to ensuring that your customers become the greatest marketing tactic you will ever employ.

Ask your customers to refer you to their friends and reward them for doing so.

Loyalty will help your customers build a sense of belonging to your brand; your community. When you reach this point, they will become your greatest advocate and you want as many advocates as possible.

SUMMARY

We are at the most critical stage now; it is time to take your customers' money. Follow through with the five selling stages and you will have done the hard work that will ensure your customers spend lots of money and want to keep coming back to do so again and again.

The five stages of sell are going to differ from retailer to retailer. You will shape them for your business as you see fit. Fortunately, much of the work that goes into them will have been established already as you've worked through the first four pillars of the successful retailer methodology. By the time you reach this stage you should know how you are going to bring them to life.

EXERCISE

Choose a pick-up piece that can be placed by the till to drive ATV at the end of a transaction.
Identify product that can be repurposed as exclusive or limited edition.
Create a voucher to handout with every online or offline sale to push a follow-on sale.

3. MEASURE

"Begin by quantifying everything related to how you do business. I mean everything. How many customers do you see in person each day? How many in the morning? In the afternoon? How many people call your business each day? How many call to ask for a price? How many want to purchase something? How many of product X are sold each day? At what time of the day are they sold? How many are sold each week? Which days are busiest? How busy? And so forth. You can't ask too many questions about the numbers."

Michael E Gerber – The E-Myth

EVERYTHING MEASURED IMPROVES

It's true. Everything measured improves. If there is a metric in your business that you are measuring every week and recording, its performance will improve. You will see it as a lever that you can pull. It will become an indicator of your business's performance.

SALES, ATV, AND PENETRATION

Start with sales. How much money did we take today compared to yesterday? Compared to the same day last week? Compared to the same day last year?

Now do this with the sales for the last week; how did that compare to the previous week? The same week last year?

Now do this for the month; how did sales compare with the same month last year?

Look at it as a percentage change rather than a cash figure.

I have talked throughout the book about the importance of improving ATV, transactions and penetration. You need to be measuring these every day, week, month, and year.

Has ATV gone up this week compared to last week? If it has gone down, you need to know why. Are you selling more of a lower-priced item that is diluting the value of your average sales?

This will be acceptable if your number of transactions has gone up and your penetration has gone up. But, without constantly measuring it you will never know if the decisions you have taken for your business are paying off.

PRODUCT PERFORMANCE

Look at your business and decide what needs measuring. If there is any part of your business that is underperforming, then create a measure by which you can assess performance and start changing things to see how the result changes.

Track your stock levels carefully; know how many items of each product are selling and how quickly, then you need never run out of a best seller. Only by watching your data like a hawk will you truly be able to accelerate your business's success.

All too often anecdotal feedback from your salespeople on what is selling well will be skewed by personal preference or individual experience. The sales data is the only measure that will give a true and accurate picture.

SET TARGETS

Staff need clear targets. Every day, every member of the team should know what their individual sales target is and what the store's target is for the day. The manager should be telling everyone throughout the day how the store is performing. All too often management keep sales performance a secret. This is nonsense. The staff can't be expected to perform if they don't know what they are going after.

ATV can be simplified for staff. Rather than telling them that yesterday the ATV was £36.21 and today we want to grow that by 7% to £38.74, tell them to focus on Units per Transaction (UPT). In my experience with my own people I've found that UPT is far easier to understand.

Increasing UPT will normally increase ATV. The exception being if you start selling lots of lower value items.

By asking everyone to make sure they sell one more item to anyone who makes a purchase then UPT and inevitably ATV will rise. But you need to be measuring this to be certain that every one of your people is doing this. They have been trained to sell; UPT is the measurement of their sales performance.

MARGIN

Look at the data from your merchandising system and analyse the margin on every product. Keep tracking your overall margin. Is margin increasing? Remember in the Product pillar we talked about watching margin like a hawk. It is critical. You need to be constantly looking to grow your margin. Set yourself a target to grow margin and track your performance along the way to ensure you achieve it. Once you have reached the target, set a new target and go again.

DON'T JUST LOOK AT TOTALS

One concept to be familiar with is that you shouldn't just add up what has happened. Totals are only interesting if compared to something or as a proportion of something.

If your sales total is 5% up on last year but 15% more people have come into your store, then are you truly improving your performance on every level? Of course not. The sales improvement is masking the decline in penetration.

Airports act as a landlord to often large numbers of retailers; the metric they are mostly interested in is income per passenger. They call this yield. It's the same in shopping centres. The landlord measures how many people walk in and the retailer provides them with their daily sales number. The yield is the total sales divided by the total visitors. This measures the performance of the shopping centre. If you remove a poor performing retailer and put in a great performing retailer the landlord will see their yield improve. I expect this to become increasingly important as landlords move towards concession fees and turnover rents. The landlord now knows the value of every single visitor. As they attract more visitors, they know what each visitor will yield.

MEASURE EVERYTHING

To truly understand your business, you need to measure everything. Constantly record and review and then set targets to improve. By measuring every aspect of your business, you will be able to focus your attention in the right areas.

Time should be set aside every week for you and your people to review performance. These measurements will tell you where the growth is coming from and critically where performance is falling away. Only with this data will you know where to focus your attention.

SUMMARY

If you were not a data geek already you will be soon. You will learn to live by your numbers. They tell you everything you need to know. The only downside is that once you start looking at data you will have a thirst for more and more.

The more things you measure, the more things you will improve. Start with ATV, UPT, penetration, sales, and margin. Then allow yourself to ask questions all over your business. Don't be afraid of data and maths if this is not your strong point. You cannot run a business without it. The good news is that the more you use it, the stronger your business will become.

You have worked hard to reach this point. All the late nights lying awake thinking about how to grow your business. Now it is payback time. All the focus has been on setting the platform to take lots of money. That is why the first four pillars are so important. Now you're ready, don't let it go to waste.

Train your people. They want to do well for themselves and they want to do well for you. Everyone likes to do a good job and it's in everyone's interest that you give them all the tools they need to do a good job.

Follow the steps to selling. Give your customers reasons to come into your store or onto your website. Make the stores look great, easy to shop, and ensure the environment is welcoming. Use promotions to drive your sales and remember that doesn't need to mean giving away margin. Your well-trained sales assistants will listen to the customer and help them to buy, and your loyalty programme will ensure they come back again.

Finally, measure your performance. Find out where you are good and strive for more. Find out where you need to do better and strive to improve. Set and share targets and measure how well you are doing.

Great sales will come if you create the environment. I have had days selling where I've been stunned by how much money my business took. By measuring what we did well before and what worked for us, by challenging my people to work in a certain way, by giving them training and targets and trusting them to do a good job, I have seen incredible things happen. These tactics absolutely work.

EXERCISE

Look at all aspects of your business and decide what you will measure.

Set targets and share them with your team.

Put time aside to review your data and set new targets.

PART 3

BRINGING IT ALL TOGETHER

The shortest chapter in any book I've read goes like this:

"Chapter 20 – On being in the right place at the right time

You are reading the wrong book. It is always the right time and this is the only place we have."

Felix Dennis – 88 The Narrow Road

Now is the time to bring everything you have learned together. If you truly desire to break through and make superb amounts of money as a retail pioneer, then you can't dodge the work that is required. The most successful retail brands, whether you like them or not, have achieved their success by being crystal clear about the strategies for each one of the pillars described in Part 2.

As I've said, there are no quick wins. In fact, having read this far you may be put off by the effort required altogether. Don't be. The juice is worth the squeeze. Be inspired by the great retail brands you see every day who are doing a remarkable job. It's been painful to reference the great work I saw Jack Wills be the exponent of over four years in light of where they are today. So many wonderful stores have been closed, people have been laid off, and great people have moved on to do incredible things elsewhere. The good news is that along the way the founders who put in the blood, sweat, and years did become successful individuals.

The 2020s will start with a deep recession. My time at Jack Wills coincided with the last global recession brought on by the banking and financial crisis, and despite the economic pressures and uncertainty, the brand grew from being a retailer with 17 stores to a household name with over 60 stores, growing into the US, Far East, and Middle East during that challenging period. I saw first-hand how the work they put into Customer, Brand, and Product paid off. As the reach and popularity of the brand grew, we began to attract the best people and recorded unprecedented sales and profits.

At any given moment, I will look at a retail business and gauge where they are on the five pillars. Where is their strength and what is their weakness? Looking at Apple I would give them 8/10 for Customer, People, and Sales, 9/10 for Brand, and 9.5/10 for Product. They are doing exceptionally well in all areas but there is a standout area for which they are rightly known. How would you gauge your business? On the scale of one to ten, where would you personally measure your business on each of the pillars? By stepping back and critically assessing each one you can see where you need to focus your efforts. I suspect you already know. Be fair on yourself. If you are passionate about your product and you know it is good, then make sure you give yourself a good score there. You've earned it. It might just be the case now that you need to share the message about how special your product is with many more people.

Working in retail is an endless strive for perfection.

Truthfully, you won't achieve it; most brilliant retailers I know are never satisfied as there is always something that needs improving.

But there will be moments when you glimpse it as being as close to perfect as you could imagine.

I can think of times where my shops have been so busy that finally at 3.30pm I run out for lunch having not eaten since 7am. I eat my sandwich across the road from the shop and watch what's happening. Stepping back and seeing the droves of customers buying my product, my carefully chosen people working hard and with smiles on their faces, truly enjoying the challenge of a busy day – those are special moments and make the work all seem worthwhile. Everything you toiled for came to this moment. Enjoy it.

BECOME A SUCCESSFUL RETAILER

Retail is simple. You buy product at one price and you sell it at a higher price. The difference between the good and the great retailers is what they do with the margin in the middle. You need to truly know and love your customer. They must inspire you and your people every day. Understanding their needs and wishes and constantly meeting and fulfilling them is your duty. Be dutiful. Find a genuine connection with your customer.

Love your brand. Care for it, nurture it, protect it. With every decision you take, reference it back to your brand. Is this on brand? Does this enhance the brand? Would our customer expect this of the brand? When the answer is yes, fill your boots. Go and do it and inspire all those who touch your brand.

As an independent retailer you cannot compete with the big chains on price. So, don't try to. Defeat them where they are at their weakest. Create outstanding product. Be the expert in your product area and ensure all your people are experts. Fight hard for your margin; the best way to make money is to increase your margin. Don't decrease it. There's only one way to go and you cannot compete down there. You can deliver value through gifts, events, great product, and excellent service.

The sooner you realise that you cannot do this on your own and that the way to make money is to harness great talent, the sooner you will achieve wonderful things. You will need to step back and trust; but rather than trust them, trust your process. Trust that you have recruited well, trained well and created an environment for your people to succeed. Your people can be your greatest asset; just give them the tools to do so.

The first four non-cash delivering pillars allow the final cash-delivering pillar to be successful. You've done all the hard work in the first four pillars, however, please don't overlook that there is still work to be done in order for the Sales pillar to be rewarding. You must apply the strategies and tactics within the Sales pillar. Bring people to your store, harness social media and your communications channels to entice them in, make the store look wonderful, and offer enticing promotions for your salespeople to leverage. Be loyal to your customers and they will be loyal to you. It will be rewarded. Then all you need to do is measure what worked well and repeat it; where something needs improving, do so.

The retailers that do this properly, that put their customer at the centre, focus their brand around the customer, create great product and select and train their people well, will drive more customers into their stores, convert more of them to make transactions, and ultimately deliver ever increasing sales.

The time is right. The time for independent retailers hasn't been better for generations. The time is now.

WILL THERE BE SHOPS IN THE FUTURE, OR WILL EVERYTHING MOVE ONLINE?

I'm asked this question a lot. The answer is yes. There will be shops in the future. The difference is that the shopping experience will improve. There will be more specialist shops with experts in their industry able to give a far more personalised experience to the customer. It's almost like we are going back 30 years but with the digital evolution laid on top. People will shop more in their own locality from shops dedicated to their craft. The butcher and baker will have their time again. Fashion will be less disposable, with talented designers now able to reach many more customers as they ally their store with the social media sites. Food retailers specialising in the narrowest of product areas will have queues outside their doors.

There will be shops, and the successful ones will be those that are part of a truly omnichannel ecosystem. Their social media, their websites, their stores all working together. All speaking to the customer with one voice.

INEDEPENDENT RETAIL IN THE 2020s – EMERGING FROM CORONAVIRUS

The coronavirus pandemic was a challenging time on so many levels. How rare it is that you can be forced to change your business model almost overnight. Yet, those that did emerged from the pandemic with a whole new way of making money. All power to them.

During the pandemic lockdown, independent retailers scurried off in several different directions.

Our local farm shop that we used to rely on for fresh food and vegetables closed its doors. Within a few days we started shopping at another nearby farm shop that set up a pre-order service. Customers were told during which 10-minute slot to turn up and collect their orders. It was simple and by the end of the lockdown we were ordering way more than at the start. Why? They had tuned into what their customer wanted. Quite simply they asked us. And if enough people asked for it, a few days later we could buy it.

Our butcher kept on trading, but we didn't use them all that often. It was the same experience as before the lockdown. They didn't try anything new to keep a captive audience spending more and more. They missed an opportunity to be more than the loyal local retailer. They could have made a significant impact by calling their customers, certainly the older ones, and putting food parcels together for them and telling them what else they could help them with. They could have put a note through everyone's doors saying what services they could deliver. The underlying message would have been clear. I'm here. I won't let you down. There's no need to socially distance with 50 other people in the big supermarket.

Our local baker was much the same. The service is often surly, and we don't think much of the bread. Because we were buying so much food from the new farm shop, we didn't even go in there for a sandwich or an iced bun like before. We queued up once at the start of the lockdown and never went back.

Hopefully after reading the five pillars of the Retail 360 methodology you can see why I was tearing my hair out at these missed opportunities. Hopefully you can see what you would have done had that been your store.

I can't abide people moaning about how trade is when they can't be bothered to go out and serve their customers in the best possible way. It doesn't take much effort to find out what your customer wants and deliver it time and again.

Perversely, one of the upsides of the pandemic was the sudden abundance of great talent in the marketplace. Have a look around, you may be surprised by the talent you can harness.

Retail is changing and we are due to see seismic change in the 2020s. Coronavirus has forced retailers to accelerate that change.

The reduction in commuting, and movements towards home or remote working will benefit local environments, particularly in traditional commuter regions outside large towns and cities. Shops, cafés and bars in city office locations will be less busy and many will close.

As customers learn that their local shops can give a better service and product than their supermarkets then they too will move away from the convenience of the big store and not mind paying a slight premium for better product with a sustainable footprint.

The next decade is set to be incredibly successful for independent retailers. There will be a move towards local stores, with a greater appreciation that product with a sustainable provenance is better than product bought en masse by large retailers. The ease of communication and media tools that are free and sit in your hand all allied with your enthusiasm for your product make this period so exciting.

MINDSET

For those who want to succeed at retail, or in fact any business, the crucial element you need is mindset. If you think the underlying messages in this book are about retail, then you have missed the point. The underlying message is about mindset. If you choose to be successful and apply the principles of becoming a successful retailer then you will be. Remember the objective: "*My objective is to become a successful retailer, to create as much profit in my business as possible, so that I can do great things for my family and make a real change in the world.*" Perhaps you have altered this and have your own objective now. Whatever it is, retail is just the industry you are in and your product is just the widget you sell.

Your mindset needs to be dedicated to achieving your objective. If you want to run a great business, then from today, and every day hereafter, you need to think and act like a great business should act. Every day decide what you are going to do, and at the end of the day review how well you have done against those goals. Ask yourself, is this how you want your business to behave?

Be a great business at whatever stage you are at. Put all five pillars in place and review how each one is performing. Only by starting as you mean to go on will you achieve your goals.

RETAIL HAS NEVER BEEN SO EXCITING

Hopefully by now you share my enthusiasm for the next decade. The opportunities for the independent retail pioneer are there to be grabbed.

Reasons to be excited:

- **Rents will drop**
- **Rates will drop and reflect business performance**
- **Customers want to shop local**
- **Big retailers will shrink in size or disappear altogether**
- **Consumers will care about provenance and sustainability**
- **Independent retailers are more agile, can take quicker decisions, and take advantage of trends**
- **Customers, particularly millennials, trust a local store far more than a national chain; independent retailers are seen as experts**
- **Millennials believe that an independent's product is more authentic and has a better provenance and supply chain than product from a large chain**
- **Millennials are turning 40 in 2020. According to Jessica Moulton from McKinsey & Company who I heard speak at a retail conference I attended in 2019, they have more cash than before, and they are 2.5x more likely to buy from an independent**

- Baby Boomers are turning 70, have retired, have cash to spend, and won't want to travel to big cities to do their shopping
- Consumers are more inclined to buy online from local retailers as they know it's simpler to take advantage of click and collect and to take back returns
- You can utilise media and the internet to reach a far wider audience than ever before
- Running your own personalised media business is cheaper and easier than ever before. You can create films on your phone, edit and add subtitles, take photos, and publish messages to an audience that you have curated and who are passionate about what you do. All from your hand-held device, all for very little investment
- You're nearly at the end of this book, you know about the five pillars and could not be better placed to become a successful retailer

FREEDOM AND DREAMS

I was 22 when I bought my first business. I would proudly tell people that I had only had nine days off all year. I worked every weekend and every hour available during the day. I was making two big mistakes.

Firstly, I was not trusting other people to do a good job. I hadn't shown them how to do so and believed I was better at doing it myself anyway. You need good people around you to succeed. Start gathering the names of people you admire. Take them out to lunch. Inspire them about what it is you are trying to do. Find out what their motivations are. When the time is right, bring them on board. They may not be unaffordable; they may be looking for a change. Equally, spend time with your own team. Find out what their motivations are; what they do when they are not at work. You could be sitting on talent you need and didn't know you had. Now, show them how to do a great job and give them the freedom and trust to do so.

Secondly, I didn't know how powerful holidays were for both me and my business. I need time on a beach to unwind. When the travel is over and the bags are unpacked, and I'm lying down on the sand staring at a cloudless sky, I finally feel the relaxation begin and I start to do my clearest thinking. I can see where I'm making mistakes and where I need to invest more time and effort. Stepping back, relaxing, and looking back is the best way to move forwards. You owe it to yourself, your family, your people, and your business.

"Great entrepreneurs take on bigger challenges. Get on and solve big challenges sooner. How big a challenge can you embrace? .... To be successful as an entrepreneur you need 3 key things: Luck, Reputation, Vitality. Wealth flows to vital people not functional people. Wealth flows to people who build a reputation and a profile. Wealth flows to people who acknowledge their luck and go out to create more of it."
Daniel Priestley – Entrepreneur Revolution

Running your independent retail business will be hard. There will be times when you look at friends taking home salaries and having weekends off. Just remember that they work within rigid rules, structures, and frameworks. None of these apply to you. You can write the rules and shape the frameworks for others. And if you don't like them you can change them. Today.

I said at the start of the book that it will be hard and that there are no silver bullets. Relax and accept this. The sooner you do, the easier it will become. Every entrepreneur I talk to has challenges to face, problems that seem insurmountable to solve. It's what makes entrepreneurs stand out that they bother to take on these challenges and find a way through or around. There always will be challenges. They just grow as your business grows. Take them on.

If you truly want something and are determined to own it or do it then you will find a way. When I needed half a million pounds to start a business I didn't stop until I had raised that money. I set the goal and achieved it. The mindset was right. I took on board all the feedback as I had knocks along the way, but I never doubted I would reach my goal.

The path to raising the half a million pounds was fascinating; only looking back can I reflect on the opportunities it created. During that journey I found myself advising the Oman Football Association on their retail strategy and sitting in their VVIP box for a critical World Cup qualifier at the invitation of a prince. A few weeks later I was a keynote speaker on the main stage of the British Business Show. My presentation on retail sandwiched between the key notes of James Caan and Caprice.

The journey is not going to be straightforward so make sure you enjoy it as you go. Celebrate the highs and reflect and learn from the lows.

We need entrepreneurs to dream. We need them to think up solutions to the greatest challenges of today. Governments cannot do it. They rarely have long enough before the next election comes around and they need to focus on winning power rather than taking on challenges that look too difficult to solve.

At the top end we see Bezos, Branson, and Musk competing to put people in space. That for them is their biggest challenge. They are doing it because it's there.

Whatever your objective is, whatever your dream is for you, your family or your chosen community, I hope you achieve it. I hope to see you there.

AFTERWORD

Everything in this book can be done by the owner of a small independent retail business. There is nothing here that is beyond your expertise or is so unaffordable it's not worth considering. I know this because I have been where you are now and because I've seen what works for the biggest, most incredibly successful retailers.

The strategic pillars in this book and the tactics within them are all deliverable in an affordable way and an achievable way. If you follow the five pillars, understand your customer, create a familiar, likeable, and trustworthy brand that talks to your customers' needs and wants with great product that your awesome people know how to sell, then you will join the ranks of successful retailers.

Most of all you will enjoy running your business because it works for you, not you for it. You will spend more time outside of your business doing the things you most enjoy with the people you most want to spend that time with. You can do this. Right now is the best time to seize the moment – go and be successful.

WE CAN HELP

I wish you the very best of luck with your retail journey. I hope you enjoy it along the way. At UK Retail Consultancy we've created ways of helping you to achieve your goals.

RETAIL 360 - THE RETAIL PIONEER PROGRAMME

Our flagship course. There is so much more that we teach on this course than I could possibly cover in this book. This programme is created for independent retailers who want to make a real change to their lives and their businesses. We deep dive into the five pillars and focus on the actual implementation of the strategies covered in this book within your business. This programme is for those who are ready to commit to improving their business and who are seeking massive growth, professional challenge, and personal transformation.

Visit: https://www.ukretailconsultancy.co.uk

FACEBOOK – RETAIL PIONEERS GROUP

Join our free online community where we share ideas and support independent retailers to grow their business. Just search for Retail Pioneers on Facebook and answer the membership questions and we'll welcome you to the group.

Visit: https://www.facebook.com/groups/retailpioneers

ACKNOWLEDGEMENTS

I have been incredibly fortunate to be supported in writing this book by so many people. It is the encouragement of so many of you that has made doing it so enjoyable. Whilst researching the book took a couple of years from idea genesis to being ready to sit down and start, the actual writing of the book took just 20 half days. That I was given the time and space to do this by my wonderful family was very generous and I will be forever grateful.

Editing the book was far harder and I would have been lost without my superb beta editors. My gorgeous sister and first reader of the book, Nikki Court, gave me such honest feedback and praise. This was so helpful and was a huge relief as I had waited on tenterhooks for a verdict. My best man and great friend, Jon Farrer, cast a keen teacher's eye over my work and spotted some howling mistakes for which I and the readers are grateful. My colleague and friend, Natalie Moren-Brown, was so generous in being both an editor and sounding board in specifics of retail; I could not have done this without your support. Helena Peacock, an old friend who is both an extraordinary copy editor and proof reader, brought the manuscript together into the book we have here today. Helena is meticulous in her work and I recommend her to anyone who needs any text reading over.

Retail is a wonderful profession. My first couple of decades in the industry have taken me to some great places and introduced me to so many remarkable people. You are all in this book somewhere. To the people I stood in fields with for many years to the people I stood in empty buildings with and dreamed of remarkable shops. All over the world we have had so much fun and I thank you for the memories.

I am fortunate to be surrounded by a great bunch of friends who know when to rib me and when to listen. Your support and enthusiasm for the book was infectious and kept me going. I fear overlooking someone but special thanks to Sophs, Joe, Jon, Alice, Jody, Toby, Pag, Woody, Marissa, Marie, Charlie, Alex, Pod, Tom, Nick, Kate, and Richard all of whom I had supportive messages and conversations with as I brought this together.

To my incredible family, so many thanks. Pops, you always listen, support, and cheer me up. Nikki, not just an incredible editor but a phenomenal mother, counsellor, and friend to us all. Tim and Rob, for so many of the stories in this book you were standing right next to me and know the successes and heartaches. You're always there and are so generous with your time and consideration. I wish you every success in your own businesses and you remain my inspiration every day. Each of you have gorgeous families who I cherish.

Finally, to my own little family; the most important people in the world. The joy of having you bundle in and see me 'in the back room' was a daily highlight that I always looked forward to. Sam, every day you came in and gave me a hug and asked how it was going. You shared in the success along the way and I look forward to doing much more of the same as we go forwards. Thank you all, xx

THE AUTHOR

RICHARD CROSS

Richard bought his first retail business at the age of 22, a failing clothing brand on the brink of liquidation which he transformed into a profitable, vertically integrated multi-channel retailer. Following that, Richard went to work for Selfridges the world's best department store and picked up the shop floor retail skills that prove so successful today.

He joined Jack Wills in 2008 as that brand set out on a momentous journey of growth. During this period, Richard opened stores across the UK, managing ever increasing teams of people before leading the business's growth in the USA and Middle East. This insight into understanding your customer and building your brand is at the heart of the strategic thinking Richard brings to life in this book.

Richard's next ventures saw him running a consultancy for independent retailers, as well as fundraising significant sums to launch and run a new retail brand and to bring a global retail brand into the UK. He became a regular keynote speaker on the main stage of the British Business Show and has since spoken about retail at events and conferences across the globe.

Richard joined a UK airport group as a consultant to advise on their retail strategies before joining them full-time to manage their retail partnerships. This experience working incredibly closely with the founders, CEOs, and business leaders of some of the greatest brands in worldwide retail, coupled with his own experience of running independent retail businesses, is brought together in this book where he showcases his personal strategy for becoming a successful retailer.

Today, Richard's passion is to help independent retailers to achieve their personal and business goals through his Retail 360 training methodology and to prove that retail is alive and well.

Printed in Great Britain
by Amazon